Strong Generative Capacity

Strong Generative Capacity
The Semantics of Linguistic Formalism

Philip H. Miller

CSLI PUBLICATIONS
Center for the Study of
Language and Information
STANFORD, CALIFORNIA

Center for the Study of Language and Information
Leland Stanford Junior University
Printed in the United States
03 02 01 00 99   5 4 3 2 1

Library of Congress Cataloging-In-Publication Data

Miller, Philip H., 1959-
Strong generative capacity : the semantics of linguistic formalism / Philip H. Miller.
p. cm. -- (CSLI lecture notes ; no. 103)
Includes bibliographical references and index.
ISBN 1-57586-213-1 (alk. paper) -- ISBN 1-57586-214-X (pbk. : alk. paper)
1. Generative grammar. 2. Semantics. 3. Grammar, Comparative and general. I. Title II. Series.

P158 .M55 1999
415--dc21

99-054248

∞ The acid-free paper used in this book meets the minimum requirements of the American National Standard for Information Sciences — Permanence of Paper for Printed Library Materials, ANSI Z39.48-1984.

Table of Contents

Preface

This research has its sources in my 'mémoire de licence' of 1983 for the Université Libre de Bruxelles. I would like to thank my advisor Marc Dominicy for his support. Our stimulating discussions at that early stage in my research crucially influenced my thinking on the subject of strong generative capacity. I would also like to acknowledge my debt to the discussion of a variety of formalisms in Levelt 1974, which initially got me interested in the idea of comparing formalisms in strong generative capacity.

This monograph was largely written in 1993 and 1994, though I have been preoccupied with the research presented in it at various times for a much longer period. For a variety of reasons, publication of the final version ended up being delayed several years during which my research projects have shifted away from the subject of mathematical linguistics. It has therefore been impossible for me to rework the manuscript in order to take into account some of the recent important developments in the field. However, I think that publication remains justified because the methods and analyses presented here are still new and relevant. I would especially like to thank Geoff Pullum for his constant support and encouragement. Without it, this book might never have been published.

Over the years, numerous friends and colleagues have influenced this work through their comments and discussion. I would like to give special thanks to Anne Abeillé, Chris Barker, Jean-Pierre Desclés, David Dowty, Gerald Gazdar, Aravind Joshi, Bob Kasper, Robert Kennes, Bill Ladusaw, Bob Levine, Louise McNally, Bruno Marchal, Michael Moortgat, Michael Niv, Carl Pollard, Geoff Pullum, Owen Rambow, and Arnold Zwicky.

Various universities and conferences gave me the opportunity to present parts of this research in talks which led to stimulating discussion and comments, namely, Université René Descartes, University of Nijmegen, Ohio State University, Université de Paris 7, University of

Pennsylvania, the 1985 and 1986 meetings of the Linguistic Society of Belgium, the Mathematical Theories of Language workshop at Stanford University in 1987, the Amsterdam Colloquium of 1993, and the 1994 meeting of the Linguistic Society of America.

I was especially fortunate to be invited to give a seminar on strong generative capacity at the 1993 LSA Linguistic Institute, at Ohio State University, where I was able to present the ideas developed here in detail. I would like to thank the organizers of the Institute for inviting me, and to thank the participants in the seminar, especially Chris Barker, David Dowty, Peter Lasersohn, Anna Maclachlan, Geoff Pullum, and Koen Versmissen, for their penetrating comments, which led to considerable improvements and new ideas in the present version.

I would also like to thank the IRIDIA laboratory of the Université Libre de Bruxelles, and specifically its director Dr. Philippe Smets, for providing me with ideal office space for my research. Working on this project would have been much more painful without the friendly and hardworking atmosphere provided by my colleagues and friends there.

This book is dedicated to the memory of my sister Marianne.

Chapter 1

Classical Definitions of Weak and Strong Generative Capacity

The notions of Weak and Strong Generative Capacity were introduced by Chomsky (1963: 325; 1965: 60). The following definition, from Chomsky 1965, is standard. "Let us say that a grammar *weakly generates* a set of sentences and that it *strongly generates* a set of structural descriptions [...]. Suppose that the linguistic theory T provides a class of grammars $G_1, G_2, ...,$ where G_i weakly generates the language L_i and strongly generates the system of structural descriptions Σ_i. Then the class $\{L_1, L_2, ...\}$ constitutes the *weak generative capacity* of T and the class $\{\Sigma_1, \Sigma_2, ...\}$ constitutes the *strong generative capacity* of T (p.60)". Defining $L(G)$ as the language generated by a grammar G and $\Sigma(G)$ as the set of structural descriptions generated by G,[1] we have:

(1) a. $\text{WGC}(G) = L(G)$
    b. $\text{WGC}(T) = \{L(G_1), L(G_2), ...\}$, where T provides $\{G_1, G_2, ...\}$

(2) a. $\text{SGC}(G) = \Sigma(G)$
    b. $\text{SGC}(T) = \{\Sigma(G_1), \Sigma(G_2), ...\}$, where T provides $\{G_1, G_2, ...\}$

These definitions immediately induce a definition of equivalence in weak and strong generative capacity (cf. Chomsky and Miller 1963: 297).

(3) a. Two grammars G_1 and G_2 are equivalent in WGC if and only if they generate the same set of strings, i.e. iff $L(G_1) = L(G_2)$.
    b. Two theories T_1 and T_2 are equivalent in WGC iff for every grammar G_i provided by T_1 there is a grammar G_i' provided by T_2 such that $L(G_i) = L(G_i')$ and for every grammar G_i'

[1] More generally, we can define $\Sigma(G)$ as the set of structural descriptions *specified* by G in order to avoid bias towards generatively oriented formalisms as opposed to acceptors or declarative formalisms.

provided by T_2 there is a grammar G_i provided by T_1 such that $L(G_i') = L(G_i)$.

(4) a. Two grammars G_1 and G_2 are equivalent in SGC if and only if they generate the same set of structural descriptions, i.e. iff $\Sigma(G_1) = \Sigma(G_2)$.

b. Two theories T_1 and T_2 are equivalent in SGC iff for every grammar G_i provided by T_1 there is a grammar G_i' provided by T_2 such that $\Sigma(G_i) = \Sigma(G_i')$ and for every grammar G_i' provided by T_2 there is a grammar G_i provided by T_1 such that $\Sigma(G_i') = \Sigma(G_i)$.

Thus, two theories are equivalent in weak (or strong) generative capacity if and only if they provide corresponding grammars that are equivalent in weak (or strong) generative capacity. On the other hand, as stated by Kuroda (1976: 307), "two grammars are strongly equivalent if they are weakly equivalent and they associate the same structural descriptions (or set of structural descriptions, in the case of ambiguity) to each string they generate".

The classical definition of strong generative capacity in (4) was first criticized by Kuroda in a series of papers (Kuroda 1973, 1976, 1987). "It is easy to see that if we limit ourselves to context-free grammars, the notion of strong equivalence is trivial. Two context-free grammars are strongly equivalent only if they are identical except for inessential details, such as the existence, in one or the other of the grammars, of rules which are not used in the derivation of terminal strings" (1976: 308). Kuroda goes on to say: "This fact, however, does not deprive the notion of strong equivalence of significance, since formal grammars, in general, can be strongly equivalent without being essentially identical" (1976: 308). Kuroda then proposes a topological approach to equivalence in SGC for context-free grammars (CFGs), based on a topological measure of tree similarity, which has had no posterity, and which I will not discuss further.

Though it is true, in some marginal cases, that formal grammars can be strongly equivalent in the classical sense without being essentially identical, I will show that the import of this fact is much more restricted than might appear here. For instance, I will argue in 3.8.1 that it is in fact illegitimate to compare derived trees in Tree Adjoining Grammars (TAGs) with derivation trees in CFGs for purposes of SGC. This crucially hinges on what entities qualify as the structural descriptions generated in a formalism.

Levelt (1974: 18-19) develops this point as follows: "The concept of 'strong equivalence' is of linguistic interest because of the problem of the descriptive adequacy of grammars. Thus if G_1 and G_2 are strongly equivalent and G_1 is descriptively adequate, then G_2 is also descriptively adequate. Yet the concept presented in its usual form is rather trivial; two strongly equivalent grammars are identical, with the possible exception of a few uninteresting details. They may only differ in unusable production rules, i.e. rules which, if used, do not lead to terminal strings, or in vocabulary elements which cannot be used. Linguistics is decidedly in need of formalization of 'equivalence of structural description', but the strength of that concept should be attuned to the tolerance of our intuitions toward syntactic structures".

It is clear that Levelt is overstating his claim, and that Kuroda is correct that, in the classical sense, two different grammars can have the same SGC. Here is a simple example. Compare the Regular Grammar G_1 which is weakly equivalent to the Tree Adjoining Grammar (TAG) G_2 (see 3.8 below for a brief description, and e.g. Joshi 1985, 1987, Joshi and Schabes 1997 for a more general introduction). Both generate trees like those in Figure 1.1.

(5) Regular Grammar G_1. $L(G_1) = \{a^*b\}$
$S \rightarrow aS,\ S \rightarrow b$

(6) Tree Adjoining Grammar G_2. $L(G_2) = \{a^*b\}$

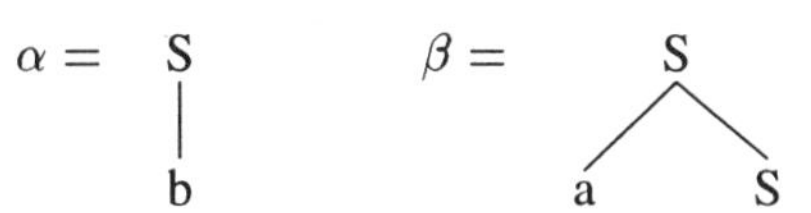

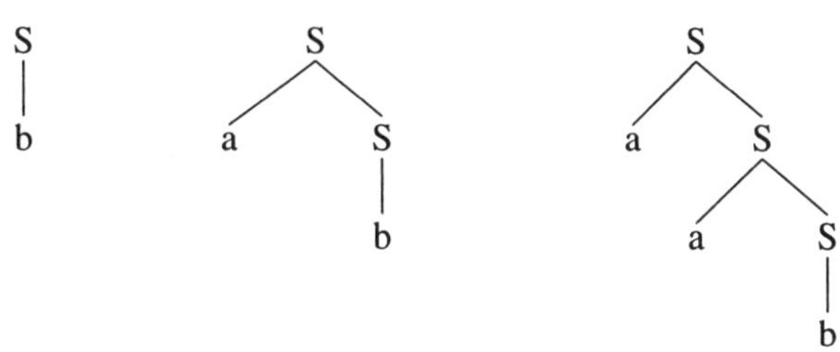

Figure 1.1

The spirit of Levelt's position is correct, however, in that such cases of equivalence are essentially irrelevant in a sense which the rest of this study will make clear. The crucially interesting point in his discussion is his idea that linguistics is in need of a concept of equivalence of structural descriptions that is more flexible than simple identity, one that should take into account our intuitions about syntactic structures. The point of the present study is to provide precisely such an analysis. Specifically, I will propose a definition of SGC as the semantic interpretation of linguistic formalism, in the classical model-theoretical sense. Structural descriptions generated by different formalisms will be interpreted in terms of abstract entities, independent of the formalisms, and designed to represent our intuitions about what it is that is claimed by assigning a certain structural description to a sentence within a given formalism. These abstract entities provide us with a level of analysis for formalisms which is more abstract than their structural descriptions, and at which a relevant comparison of the formalisms is possible, even if they use crucially different notations

Returning to the discussion of the above example in this perspective, it turns out that it is in fact undesirable to consider the phrase structure trees generated by a TAG as their structural descriptions. Indeed, the phrase structure trees do not allow us to capture the crucial intuitive interpretation, suggested by those working in the TAG framework, according to which certain subparts of the tree are elementary tree structures. In fact, as will be justified in 3.8, the structural descriptions of TAGs should not be take to be the 'derived trees' (as in Figure 1.1), but more abstract and more informative structures called 'derivation trees', which express this intuitively relevant interpretation. In general, we will require the structural description of a string to be an entity expressing all of the relevant structural information that the formalism attributes to the string (cf. 3.8 for further discussion). Consequently, our analysis will in fact vindicate Levelt's intuition concerning the trivial nature of the classical definition of strong equivalence.

The intuition that SGC should be defined in terms of a notion of 'equivalence of structural description' that is weaker than simple identity has been shared by many mathematical linguists.[2] However, in general,

---

[2] Note though that the strictly classical definition in terms of identity remains the most frequent, e.g. "If [...] two grammars generate the same language by means of the same tree structures [...], then the two grammars are said to be *strongly equivalent*" (Berwick and Weinberg 1984: 8). "[Grammars] G_1 and G_2 are *strongly equivalent* if they are weakly equivalent and for each w in $L(G_1) = L(G_2)$, G_1 and G_2 assign the same structural description to w" (Joshi 1985: 207).

no explicit definition of what constitutes equivalence is provided.[3] Kornai and Pullum 1990 suggest isomorphism between structural descriptions as a criterion for strong equivalence.[4] However, they provide no specification of what functions or relations should be preserved under the isomorphic mapping, depriving the definition of any formal content. Furthermore, even if a set of functions or relations to be preserved was defined, we would only have a definition for *equivalence* in SGC. The concept of SGC itself would still lack an appropriate analysis beyond the classical notion of sets of structural descriptions generated.

One major exception to this naïve stance on SGC appears in the work of Joshi and his collaborators (e.g. Weir 1988, Joshi, Vijay-Shanker and Weir 1991, Rambow, Becker and Niv 1992, Rambow 1994). As Weir (1988: 4) points out : "The problem with comparing the strong generative capacity of different formalisms and making general statements about how the strong generative capacity should be limited is that such criteria should be applicable to a range of radically different systems. Such criteria have been difficult to develop as, for example, the objects comprising the grammar (e.g., productions or trees), and the structural descriptions (e.g., trees, graphs) could be very different notationally". One of Weir's objectives is to develop explicit and more powerful criteria for evaluating the SGC of grammatical formalisms. However, his direction of research is rather different from the one adopted here. His methods and results will be compared to those presented here in the final concluding chapter.

Let me conclude this review with the following quote: "The concept of strong generative capacity does not help since (a) there is no hierarchy in terms of which to measure it and (b) it is not altogether clear how to compare the strong generative capacities of linguistically significant models such as government-binding grammar, generalized phrase structure grammar, lexical-functional grammar, and the like. Although many of these models give sets of labeled phrase structure trees, there generally is information produced from these trees which

---

[3] As for instance in "Two grammars [...] are strongly equivalent if they [...] assign equivalent structural descriptions (under *some* definition of equivalence) [my emphasis, PHM]" (GKPS 1985: 43).

[4] "The resulting [...] grammar will be not only weakly equivalent to the original one but also strongly equivalent (at least if isomorphism between structural descriptions is taken as the criterion for strong equivalence)" (Kornai and Pullum 1990: 28).

differs from model to model" (Rounds, Manaster-Ramer and Friedman 1987: 351).

The purpose of this study is to provide a definition of SGC which is not subject to these criticisms and which is both useful and operational. For this to be the case, we must overcome the problem of the incommensurability of the sets of structural descriptions specified by different formalisms, and provide appropriate hierarchies for evaluating SGC. Furthermore, we must provide an analysis of SGC which corresponds to the basic intuition which linguists share about it, namely that it should be a characterization of the expressive power of a formalism, a characterization of what it is that the formalism claims about a string when it is generated with a given structural description. In other words, we require a semantically based conception of SGC.

Chapter 2

Constituency, Dependency, Labeling and Ordering

2.1 Equivalence in Strong Generative Capacity in Terms of Isomorphisms

As mentioned in the preceding chapter, using the notion of isomorphism between sets of structural descriptions can provide a solution to the problem of incommensurability faced by the classical definition of SGC, when it is applied to formalisms specifying different types of structural descriptions. Under this approach, two grammars G and G' are equivalent in SGC if there is an isomorphism between their derivation sets i.e. a bijective mapping which preserves certain given functions or relations:

> SGC(G) = SGC(G') iff, for the functions or relations $f_1, ..., f_n$ on $\Sigma(G)$ and the corresponding functions or relations $f_1', ..., f_n'$ on $\Sigma(G')$, there is a bijective mapping ϕ, $\phi: \Sigma(G) \rightarrow \Sigma(G')$, such that
>
> if $\phi(D_i) = D_i'$, $D_i \in \Sigma(G)$ and $D_i' \in \Sigma(G')$,
> then, for all j, $1 \leq j \leq n, f_j(D_i) = f_j'(D_i')$.

This is illustrated in Figure 2.1.

Though this idea solves the incommensurability problem, it provides us only with a notion of equivalence in SGC, rather than with an appropriate analysis of the concept of SGC itself. Furthermore, it leaves open the crucial question of which functions or relations should be preserved by the bijective mapping ϕ.

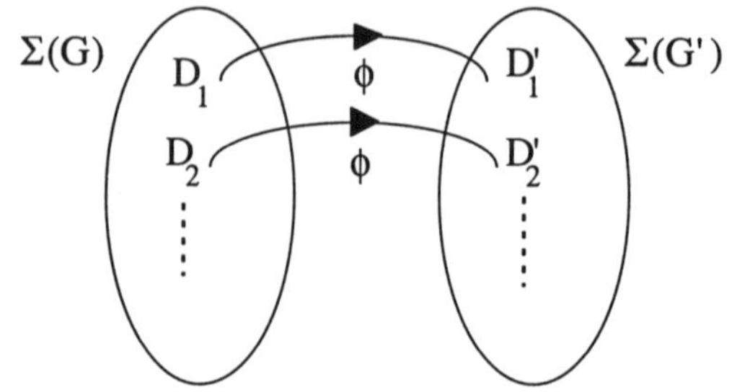

Figure 2.1

2.2 Relevant Functions and Relations

In order to understand what is at stake in the choice of functions and relations to be preserved by the isomorphic mapping, a detour through elementary arithmetic will be useful. Elementary arithmetic in base 10 and base 9 are isomorphic (arithmetical functions, relations, and operations are preserved under a bijective mapping between the representations of the numbers in any two bases). But not everything is preserved. For instance, finiteness of representation of rational numbers in decimal notation is not preserved:

(1)		Base 10		Base 9
$1/2$	=	0.5	=	0.444...
$1/3$	=	0.333...	=	0.3

The reason why mathematicians consider arithmetic in different bases to be equivalent, despite this instance of non-preservation, is that the finiteness of decimal representations is not an arithmetical property of rational numbers. It is simply a property of the representations and has no relevant interpretation with respect to to the entities modeled. Arithmetic in different bases is equivalent because all *relevant* arithmetical properties are preserved. Thus, in any discussion of equivalence in terms of isomorphisms, there is a crucial notion of *relevance* of aspects of the representation which is grounded in the *intended interpretations* of the representations. More generally, the question of which functions and relations are relevant, and should be preserved by the isomorphism in order to show equivalence, can only be answered by analyzing the intended interpretations of the formalism, i.e. what the users of the formalism consider it to express. Two caveats are in order here: (a) It will be shown in 2.15 that in some cases certain intended interpretations are illegitimate, given the way in which a formalism is defined. In such cases, it is sometimes possible to redefine the formalism so as to make the interpretation legitimate (cf. section 2.1.4 below for a discussion of the legitimacy of dependency interpretations for CFGs). (b) It is possible to discuss the question of whether a given formalism legitimately supports an interpretation, independently of the intended interpretations of the formalism by its conceptors and/or users. For instance, it is possible to discuss whether or not a Dependency Grammar supports a legitimate constituent structure interpretation, independently of whether or not users of the theory intend it to (cf. below 2.12).

Our discussion of the use of isomorphisms to define equivalence in SGC thus leads to an important insight. When analyzing the expressive power of a formalism, we must systematically distinguish those aspects of the formalism which are intended to be relevant from those which are not. Building on this insight, we now introduce a semantically based technique for analyzing SGC itself, rather than directly defining equivalence in SGC.

2.3 Interpretation Domains: the Case of Constituent Structure

In order to characterize the SGC of a formalism in semantical terms, we need to be able to specify explicitly what it is that is claimed about a given string when a grammar written in that formalism generates that string with a certain structural description.[1] That is, we must be able to specify which are the intended interpretations of a structural description in a given formalism. For this purpose we introduce the notion of *Interpretation Domain.* Interpretation Domains are set up to provide explicit characterizations of linguistically significant properties of sentences, independently of specific formalisms. For explicitness and ease of manipulation, we define them in set-theoretic terms.

Perhaps the most intuitive way of clarifying the notion of Interpretation Domain is through a simple example. Constituent structure (or constituency) is one of the properties that is most frequently a relevant intended interpretation of linguistic formalisms. In

---

[1] For present purposes, we can identify the concept of *structural description* assigned to a sentence by a grammar with that of *derivation* of a sentence in a grammar. See 3.8 below for further discussion.

most formalisms, one of the things that a structural description specifies about a string is its constituent structure. For instance, any syntactic formalism necessarily makes the minimal assumption that the objects which it identifies as syntactic words in a sentence are constituents of that sentence. Furthermore, as will appear below, other classical interpretations of linguistic formalisms, such as dependency and endocentricity, implicitly define a constituent structure interpretation beyond the minimal one just mentioned, though the opposite is not true. This asymmetry clearly shows the fundamental status of constituent structure in linguistic theory.[2] We can define a constituent structure on a set of occurrences of linguistic units in a completely general way as follows.

Consider a vocabulary V (e.g., if we are modeling syntax, V will be a set of syntactic words). Let S be a set of occurrences of elements of V (i.e. a set of pairs $\langle v, i \rangle$ where v belongs to V and i is an index and there are no two pairs $\langle v, i \rangle$ and $\langle v', j \rangle$ in S such that $i = j$).[3] A *constituent structure* Γ on S is a set of non-empty subsets of S.[4] This gives us the most abstract conceivable definition of constituency:

- No ordering relation is imposed on the occurrences.
- Nothing forces the whole set of occurrences to form a constituent, nor each individual occurrence to form a constituent.
- There are no constraints on overlapping constituents.

It can thus characterize theories allowing unordered constituents, discontinuous constituency and multidominance (cf. 4.2), syncategorematic occurrences (cf. 2.5.2), and non-connected constituent structures (cf. Marcus et al. 1983).

We can define the Interpretation Domain for constituency (ID_C) as

---

[2] Cf. Milner (1989: 269ff) for an extensive theoretical discussion of the central status of constituency at all levels of linguistic theorizing and Miller 1992, chapter 1, for a critical discussion of the status of classical constituency tests in syntax.

[3] Technically, S is an *indexed set*, i.e. a function from the natural numbers to V. This definition is similar to that of a *multiset* in that it allows for more than one occurrence of a given element of the vocabulary in a set. But the present definition allows us to make distinct reference to elements occurring more than once (e.g. $\langle a, 2 \rangle$ can be distinguished from $\langle a, 3 \rangle$, which is not possible under the classical definition of multiset.

[4] This is a generalization of the definition of constituent structure given in Gladkii (1970: 10), who includes the constraints given in (4) below directly in the definition of constituent structure.

the set of sets of subsets of this type, i.e. the set of abstract characterizations of constituency in the most general terms. Note that this definition is strictly set theoretic and is completely independent of any specific formalism. We can now specify what constituent structure is intended for a string which is assigned a certain structural description in a given formalism by exhibiting the corresponding element of ID_C.

Technical note. More specifically, we define the elements of ID_C as the pairs $\langle I, \Gamma \rangle$, where I is a set of indices and Γ is a constituent structure on I, i.e. a set of non-empty subsets of I. This is necessary for two reasons. First, in order to be able to characterize arbitrary constituent structures on a set of indices, we need to specify that set, since in the general case it is not necessary for all indices in I to appear in the subsets Γ. When the set of indices is obvious given Γ, we will only note the constituent structure Γ, for simplicity. Second, we need to refer to indices, rather than occurrences if we want to be able to characterize constituent structures independently of the specific elements that occur in them. This allows us to claim that two different sets of occurrences can have the same constituent structure, and more generally, that relabeling the vocabulary of items that occur does not change the properties of a system in terms of constituency. The notion of constituent structure on a set of occurrences (as defined above in the main text, and which we will often use below for simplicity) is equivalent to the pairing of a constituent structure on a set of indices with an assignment of vocabulary items to indices. Note furthermore that we can partition ID_C into equivalence classes where each class contains all of the constituent structures on a set I of cardinality n which are identical up to permutations of natural numbers within I. We will consider all constituent structures in such an equivalence class to be identical.

2.4 Interpretation Functions

Given a certain Interpretation Domain and a certain formalism which is intended to represent properties characterized by that Interpretation Domain, we want a general procedure to specify which element of the Interpretation Domain corresponds to a given structural description. This will be done by providing an *Interpretation Function* for the formalism. Specifically, an Interpretation Function is a function which associates a structural description in a given formalism with its interpretation in a given Interpretation Domain. These functions are consequently doubly specific: for each Interpretation Domain, we need an Interpretation Function for each formalism. We note the Interpretation Function mapping derivations in the formalism T into the Interpretation Domain ID as $IF_{T \rightarrow ID}$. In cases where the choice of T is obvious, we will not always note it explicitly.

As a simple example, let us consider the Interpretation Function for constituent structure for CFGs viz. $IF_{CFG \rightarrow C}$. This function maps derivations in CFGs to the Interpretation Domain for constituency, ID_C. $IF_{CFG \rightarrow C}$ will map the derivation in Figure 2.2 to the constituent structure Γ in ID_C, given in (2).[5]

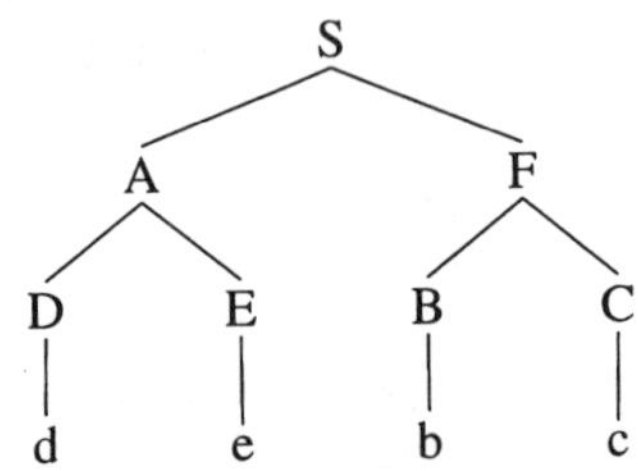

Figure 2.2

(2) $\Gamma = \{\{\langle d, 1\rangle, \langle e, 2\rangle, \langle b, 3\rangle, \langle c, 4\rangle\}; \{\langle d, 1\rangle, \langle e, 2\rangle\}; \{\langle b, 3\rangle, \langle c, 4\rangle\}; \{\langle d, 1\rangle\}; \{\langle e, 2\rangle\}; \{\langle b, 3\rangle\}; \{\langle c, 4\rangle\}\}$

Technically, $IF_{CFG \rightarrow C}$ can be defined as in (3), where σ denotes a structural description in $\Sigma(CFG)$.

(3) $IF_{CFG \rightarrow C} : \Sigma(CFG) \rightarrow ID_C: \sigma \rightarrow \Gamma$ such that for all occurrences of A in σ, $A \in V_N$, the set of occurrences of elements of V_T dominated by A belongs to Γ.

2.5 Advantages of the Approach

The analysis of SGC sketched above has three major advantages.

---

[5] Note that the assignment of indices to occurrences chosen in (2) is arbitrary; any other choice would have led to an equivalent statement of the constituent structure in the sense of the technical note at the end of 2.3. Namely, any other choice would be in the same equivalence class. Note also that the choice of indices has no interpretation here in terms of the ordering of the occurrences in the string.

2.5.1 Explicitness

First, it allows us to characterize explicitly the subset of an Interpretation Domain which can be represented by a given grammar or theory. This is essentially what we will be defining as the SGC of the grammar or theory with respect to that Interpretation Domain in Chapter 3. For instance, we can define the subset of ID_C which can be represented by CFGs, given the Interpretation Function in (3). CFGs are able to generate all and only structural descriptions such that their constituent structure interpretations satisfy the conditions in (4).[6] The subset of ID_C satisfying conditions (4) is the union of the SGCs of all CFGs, $IF_{CFG \to C}(\Sigma(CFG))$, using the definitions to be given in Chapter 3.

(4) a. S belongs to Γ; and
    b. If E_1 and E_2 belong to Γ, and the intersection of E_1 and E_2 is not empty, then :
        E_1 is included in E_2; or
        E_2 is included in E_1.

Condition (4a) accounts for the fact that in any derivation in a CFG the set S of all the occurrences in the string generated is a constituent, since it is dominated by the root node. Condition (4b) rules out overlapping constituents and multidominance.[7]

2.5.2 Alternate Definitions

Second, this approach makes it possible to provide alternate definitions of the intended interpretations assigned to a given structural description. In their full generality, CFGs (as defined e.g. in Chomsky 1963) allow structural descriptions of the types shown for example in Figures 2.3 and 2.4, where the items *b* and *c* are said to be *syncategorematic*, i.e. not assigned to a nonterminal category.[8]

---

[6] This definition is similar to that of *ramification* (Gaifman 1965: 313). Note however that Gaifman's definition forces all occurrences to be constituents.

[7] Note that we are unable, at this stage, to characterize the 'no crossing branches' constraint on derivations in CFGs, because ID_C does not characterize the ordering properties of occurrences. See 2.7 below for a statement of this constraint.

[8] It is possible to find explicit usage of syncategorematic lexical items in linguistic analyses, e.g. in the famous rule *Aux → C (M) (have + en) (be + ing)* of Chomsky (1957: 39), where *have*, *en*, *be* and *ing* are syncategorematic.

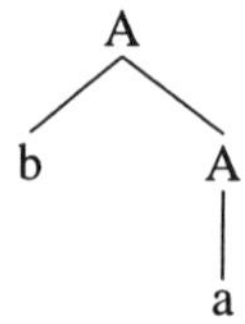

Figure 2.3

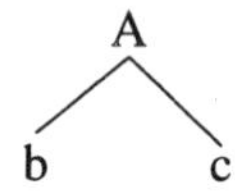

Figure 2.4

Different choices are possible as to the constituency defined by such structures. According to the Interpretation Function chosen in (3), the item *b* in Figure 2.3 and the items *b* and *c* in Figure 2.4 will not form constituents, since there is no nonterminal which dominates them without dominating other terminals. But we could just as well choose alternate Interpretation Functions for characterizing the constituency defined by CFGs if this result is not considered to be the desired interpretation in such cases. For instance, we can decide that trees like those above should be interpreted as claiming that the occurrences of *b* and *c* do form constituents on their own. An Interpretation Function giving such results is provided in (5):

(5) $IF_{CFG \rightarrow C}$ (revised): $\Sigma(CFG) \rightarrow ID_C$: $\sigma \rightarrow \Gamma$ such that
  (i) for all occurrences of A in σ, $A \in V_N$, the set of occurrences of elements of V_T dominated by A belongs to Γ; and
  (ii) for all occurrences $\langle a, i \rangle$ in σ, $a \in V_T$, the singleton $\{\langle a, i \rangle\}$ belongs to Γ.

This choice for the Interpretation Function $IF_{CFG \rightarrow C}$, which we will make in the rest of this study, enforces the idea that any syntactic word forms a syntactic constituent, whether or not it is assigned a category, causing us to revise (4) by adding (4c):

(4) c. For all occurrences $\langle v, i \rangle$ belonging to S, $\{\langle v, i \rangle\}$ belongs to Γ.

As a second example, if one takes seriously the proposal by Chomsky (1986: 7), following May 1985, according to which, in an adjunction structure such as $[_\beta\ \alpha\ [_\beta\ ...]]$, the occurrence of α is not dominated by the higher occurrence of β, one might want to change the Interpretation Function for constituency so that such a structure does not define a constituent consisting of those items dominated by α and those dominated by the lower occurrence of β.[9]

More generally, as we will see below, there are formalisms where different constituency interpretations for the structural descriptions are equally plausible a priori. Our usage of explicit Interpretation Functions allows us to formulate precisely the different possibilities, and to study their consequences.

2.5.3 General Applicability

Third, defining explicit Interpretation Functions, rather than relying on intuitive means, makes it possible to define constituent structure interpretations for systems for which constituent structure may not be an obvious property, e.g. Combinatory Categorial Grammars, String Adjunct Grammars or Dependency grammars.

2.6 Labeled Constituent Structure

In the rest of this chapter, I will define various simple Interpretation Domains and illustrate them with respect to simple grammatical formalisms. The definition of the Interpretation Domain for constituency given in 2.3 does not allow for a characterization of the category labeling of constituents. This is however a classical and important intended interpretation for many grammatical formalisms with constituency interpretations. We can define the Interpretation Domain for labeled constituent structures $\mathrm{ID_{LC}}$ as the set of pairs $\langle\Gamma, L\rangle$, where Γ is a constituent structure and L is a relation between the constituents in Γ and a set of labels LABEL. The Interpretation Function for CFGs into $\mathrm{ID_{LC}}$ is trivial to state, given the obvious intended interpretations of the formalism:

(6) $\mathrm{IF_{CFG\rightarrow LC}} : \Sigma(\mathrm{CFG}) \rightarrow \mathrm{ID_{LC}}: \sigma \rightarrow \langle\Gamma, L\rangle$ such that

a. for all occurrences of A in σ, $A \in V_N$, the set M of occurrences of elements of V_T dominated by A belongs to Γ and $\langle M, A\rangle$ is in L; and

[9] For instance, one could add the condition 'such that A does not directly dominate another occurrence of A' to (3), resulting in:

(i) $\mathrm{IF_{CFG\rightarrow C}}$ (revised 2): $\Sigma(\mathrm{CFG}) \rightarrow \mathrm{ID_C}: \sigma \rightarrow \Gamma$ such that for all occurrences of A in σ, $A \in V_N$ and A does not directly dominate another occurrence of A, the set of occurrences of elements of V_T dominated by A belongs to Γ.

b. for all occurrences $\langle a, i\rangle$ in σ, $a \in V_T$, the singleton $\{\langle a, i\rangle\}$ belongs to Γ and if there is no B, $B \in V_N$, such that B exclusively dominates $\{\langle a, i\rangle\}$, then $\{\langle a, i\rangle\}$ is not related to a label by L.

In effect, every constituent will be labeled by the label of the node dominating it, except for syncategorematic terminals which will bear no label.[10] For Figures 2.2, 2.3, and 2.4, we obtain the labeled constituent structures (7a, b, c) respectively:

(7) a. $\Gamma = \{\{\langle d, 1\rangle, \langle e, 2\rangle, \langle b, 3\rangle, \langle c, 4\rangle\}; \{\langle d, 1\rangle, \langle e, 2\rangle\}; \{\langle b, 3\rangle, \langle c, 4\rangle\}; \{\langle d, 1\rangle\}; \{\langle e, 2\rangle\}; \{\langle b, 3\rangle\}; \{\langle c, 4\rangle\}\}$

$L = \{\langle\{\langle d, 1\rangle, \langle e, 2\rangle, \langle b, 3\rangle, \langle c, 4\rangle\}, S\rangle; \langle\{\langle d, 1\rangle, \langle e, 2\rangle\}, A\rangle; \langle\{\langle b, 3\rangle, \langle c, 4\rangle\}, F\rangle; \langle\{\langle d, 1\rangle\}, D\rangle; \langle\{\langle e, 2\rangle\}, E\rangle; \langle\{\langle b, 3\rangle\}, B\rangle; \langle\{\langle c, 4\rangle\}, C\rangle\}$

b. $\Gamma = \{\{\langle b, 1\rangle, \langle a, 2\rangle\}, \{\langle b, 1\rangle\}, \{\langle a, 2\rangle\}\}$

$L = \{\langle\{\langle b, 1\rangle, \langle a, 2\rangle\}, A\rangle, \langle\{\langle a, 2\rangle\}, A\rangle\}$

c. $\Gamma = \{\{\langle b, 1\rangle, \langle c, 2\rangle\}, \{\langle b, 1\rangle\}, \{\langle c, 2\rangle\}\}$

$L = \{\langle\{\langle b, 1\rangle, \langle c, 2\rangle\}, A\rangle\}$

A caveat is in order here as to my use of the term *labeling*, which should not be confused with the classical definition of labeling of a tree. The latter considers a tree to be a set of nodes which are labeled by either terminals (leaf nodes) or nonterminals (other nodes). Here, I am considering labels as denoting types of constituents. Consequently, only constituents bear labels. Individual occurrences of items (in the case of the syntactically oriented examples we have been using here, lexical items) are not interpreted as labels.[11]

---

[10] Note that given this choice of Interpretation Function, a non-branching structure of type $[_A [_B x]]$, will lead to the set of occurrences x being labeled as both an A and a B by L (this is what prevents making L a function from constituents to labels). Furthermore, the Interpretation Function chosen here does not preserve dominance properties of the CF derivation in non-branching structures, viz. $[_A [_B x]]$ and $[_B [_A x]]$ are mapped to the same labeled constituent structure. Note that this is not an a priori implausible interpretation of the formalism, though it is clearly not the only one possible.

[11] Note that this way of analyzing labeling can be understood to directly enforce the Principle of Phonology Free Syntax of Zwicky and Pullum 1986. Indeed, the label (in the classical sense) of a leaf node (i.e. a lexical item understood here as its phonological representation) is not interpreted as relevant syntactic labeling

2.7 Linear Order

Our discussion of the intended interpretation of structural descriptions for CFGs up to this point has ignored one crucial point, namely the ordering of terminals, and derivatively of the constituents containing them. We can define an Interpretation Domain for linear order, ID_O, in the following way. Elements of this domain are sets of occurrences, where, contrary to what we have been doing up to now, we interpret the indexation of occurrences in terms of ordering. We define ID_O as the set of such sets of occurrences. For example, the obvious Interpretation Function $IF_{CFG \to O}$ for CFGs maps Figure 2.2 above to (8) in ID_O:

(8) $\{\langle d, 1\rangle, \langle e, 2\rangle, \langle b, 3\rangle, \langle c, 4\rangle\}$

It is important to note that interpretations in terms of ordering and of constituency are not independent for CFGs. Specifically, condition (9) holds for all structural descriptions generated by CFGs.

(9) If a structural description σ generated by a CFG is assigned an interpretation $i_o \in ID_O$ by $IF_{CFG \to O}$, $i_o = \{\langle x_i, i\rangle, 1 \leq i \leq n\}$, then, for every set E in Γ, $\Gamma \in ID_C$ and $\Gamma = IF_{CFG \to C}(\sigma)$, (i.e. Γ is the interpretation of σ in terms of constituency), E is a continuous substring of i_o.

Condition (9) in fact states the inability of CFGs to express discontinuous constituency. More generally, we can state the following theorem:

(10) CFGs are able to express all and only the pairs of interpretations in terms of constituency and ordering satisfying both (4a, b, c) and (9).

This dependency holding between ordering and constituency interpretations for CFGs is a typical example of the fact that there are constraints on the possible pairings of interpretations in different domains expressible by a single structural description within a given formalism. Our definitions of SGC in Chapter 3 will be specifically designed to take interdependencies of this kind into account. Note also, that it is trivial to define a single Interpretation Domain ID_{OC} expressing constituency and order at the same time: one needs only to consider the

---

information and will consequently not be accessible to syntactic conditions or operations.

ordering of indices in ID_C as significant to get the desired result. More generally, for any number of Interpretation Domains $ID_1, ..., ID_n$, it is always possible to obtain a new Interpretation Domain, which subsumes their combined expressive power, by taking their Cartesian product $ID_1 \times ... \times ID_n$.

2.8 An Interpretation Domain for Dependency

The idea of dependency relations between occurrences in a string is a classical one in syntax, dating back at least to 18th century syntactic theories (cf. Dominicy 1982), and transmitted to 20th century linguistics through e.g. Tesnière 1959. The tradition of dependency based syntax is especially vigorous in European linguistics, cf. e.g. Hudson 1984, Mel'čuk and Pertsov 1987, etc. Moreover, the directly related notion of headedness has become crucial in current mainstream syntax with the success of X-bar theory.

Let us define a dependency relation on a set of occurrences S as a relation R on the occurrences of S, $R = \{\langle i, j\rangle, ...\}$, $i, j \in S$, where the presence of the pair $\langle i, j\rangle$ in R is interpreted as meaning that occurrence i in S depends on occurrence j. This is illustrated in (11).

(11)

$R = \{\langle\text{the, girl}\rangle, \langle\text{girl, spoke}\rangle, \langle\text{her, mother}\rangle, \langle\text{mother, to}\rangle, \langle\text{to, spoke}\rangle\}$[12]

Note that we are defining dependency relations on sets of occurrences, rather than on strings. In considering such structures to be crucially unordered, we are following a common practice among dependency theorists, cf. e.g. Mel'čuk and Pertsov 1987. As was done above for constituent structures, linear ordering properties will be interpreted separately. We define ID_D as the set of all such relations on sets of occurrences.

Technical Note. As was the case for constituent structures, we specifically define the elements of ID_D as pairs $\langle I, D\rangle$ the first element of which is a set of indices, and the second a dependency relation on that set. This is crucial for the same reasons as those discussed at the end of

---

[12] Because there is only one occurrence of each item, it is possible here, for simplicity, not to note indices explicitly.

section 2.3, namely, (a) it allows dependency relations where not all the indices in the set I are involved; and (b) it makes it possible to characterize dependency relations independently of the specific elements that occur in them. A dependency relation on a set of occurrences, as defined in the text above, is equivalent to the pairing of a dependency relation on a set of indices and an assignment of vocabulary items to the indices.

We can define indirect dependence as follows: an occurrence i indirectly depends on an occurrence k if there are occurrences $j_1, ..., j_n$, $n \geq 0$ such that i depends on j_1, j_1 depends on j_2, ..., j_{n-1} depends on j_n, and j_n depends on k. Thus, in (11), the occurrence of *mother* indirectly depends on the occurrence of *spoke*, though it does not directly depend on it.[13]

Note also that we can define on the basis of this notion of dependency, which holds between occurrences, a notion of dependency between constituents and occurrences, which we will call *c-dependency*. If R is a dependency relation between occurrences, then we define the corresponding c-dependency relation R' as the set of pairs $\langle S, j \rangle$ such that $\langle i, j \rangle$ is in R and S is the set of occurrences depending directly or indirectly on i. The relation R' for (11) is given in (12).

(12) {⟨{the}, girl⟩, ⟨{the, girl}, spoke⟩, ⟨{her}, mother⟩, ⟨{her, mother}, to⟩, ⟨{to, her, mother}, spoke⟩}

Finally, we can define the *head-of* relation on the basis of the notion of dependency between occurrences: an occurrence is the head of the constituent comprising itself together with all of the occurrences which depend on it directly or indirectly. Specifically we define head-of relations as sets of pairs $\langle j, S \rangle$ where S is a set of occurrences comprising j and all the occurrences depending directly or indirectly on j. The head-of relation for (11) is given in (13).

(13) {⟨the, {the}⟩, ⟨girl, {the, girl}⟩, ⟨spoke, {the, girl, spoke, to, her, mother}⟩, ⟨to, {to, her, mother}⟩, ⟨mother, {her, mother}⟩, ⟨her, {her}⟩}

All these relations are interdefinable, and any one of them could have been chosen as the basis for the Interpretation Domain ID_D.

---

[13] In general, I simply use *depend*, as defined above, for direct dependence, but I will sometimes use the more explicit *directly depend* when there is a possibility of confusion.

2.9 Simple Dependency Grammars

We will now review a simple grammatical formalism, classical dependency grammars, which has dependency as its central intended interpretation. Following e.g. Hays 1964, Gaifman 1965 and Robinson 1970, we define a dependency grammar DG as a 5-tuple $\langle V_N, V_T, D, L, T \rangle$, where

- V_N, the nonterminal vocabulary, and V_T, the terminal vocabulary, are finite sets;
- D is a finite set of Dependency Rules;
- L is a finite set of Lexical rules; and
- $T \in V_N$ is the initial symbol.

Dependency rules indicate for each category in V_N, which categories in V_N can depend on it, and their relative position. They are of the following form, (14b) being a special case of (14a).

(14) a. $B\,(A_1, ..., A_n * C_1, ..., C_m)$ $\qquad n, m \geq 0$
 b. $B(*)$

Rule (14a) means that an occurrence of the category B can have nodes A_1, ..., A_n as dependents on its left, in that order, and C_1, ..., C_m as dependents on its right, in that order.[14] Rule (14b) means that an occurrence of category B can appear without any dependents.

Lexical rules are simple rewriting rules of the form $A \rightarrow a$, where $A \in V_N$ and $a \in V_T$, indicating which terminal items are assigned to each nonterminal category.

Derivations start with the initial symbol T, and are terminated when the two following conditions are fulfilled: (i) For every nonterminal without a nonterminal daughter there is a rule of type (14b) in the grammar; (ii) all nonterminals have been rewritten as terminals by a lexical rule. Gaifman 1965 (theorem 3.11) proves that DGs and CFGs are equivalent in weak generative capacity.

The following example illustrates the way DGs work.

D = {V(N*P), P(*N), N(Det*), Det(*)}
L = {V → spoke, N → girl, mother, P → to, Det → the, her}
V_N = {V, N, P, Det} where V is the initial symbol.

This grammar generates the sentence *the girl spoke to her mother*

---

[14] Note that the asterisk in (14a, b) is not the Kleene star. It marks the position of the lexical head in the string of dependents.

assigning it the derivation in Figure 2.5. The dependency relation expressed by this structure is given in (11) repeated here as (15).

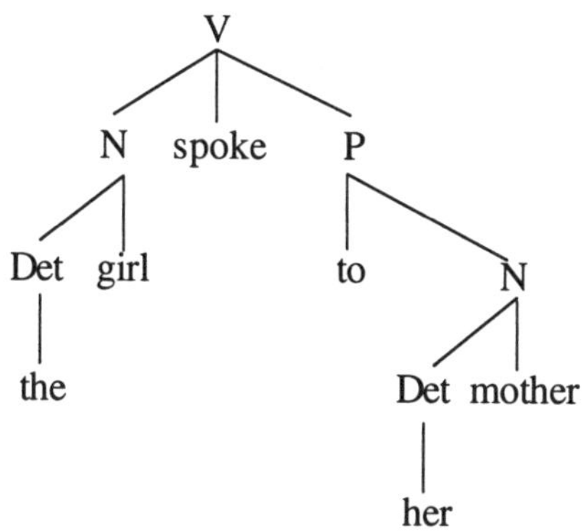

Figure 2.5

(15) 

R = {⟨the, girl⟩, ⟨girl, spoke⟩, ⟨her, mother⟩, ⟨mother, to⟩, ⟨to, spoke⟩}

2.10 An Interpretation Function for Dependency for DGs

We can define an Interpretation Function to dependency relations for DGs, $IF_{DG \rightarrow D}$, as follows:

(16) $IF_{DG \rightarrow D} : \Sigma(DG) \rightarrow ID_D: \sigma \rightarrow R$ such that R includes all and only the pairs of occurrences $\langle j, k \rangle$ such that k is the lexical daughter of the grandmother of j in σ.

This definition allows us to specify the subset of ID_D which is expressible by DGs as in theorem (17) (cf. Gaifman 1965: 306). The proof of these properties is obvious, given the definition of the Interpretation Function.

(17) DGs can express all and only the dependency relations R such that R is an irreflexive, asymmetric, intransitive relation on a set of occurrences, and such that (a) there is one and only one occurrence

which does not depend on any other occurrence; (b) every other occurrence depends on one and only one occurrence.

2.11 Ordering Properties of DGs

Beyond assigning a dependency interpretation to a set of occurrences, some proponents of dependency oriented grammatical formalisms assume that an ordering interpretation is also relevant (e.g. Hays 1964, Gaifman 1965, Robinson 1970). To obtain such an interpretation, we can interpret the indexation of occurrences in terms of ordering, as in 2.7. Simple DGs, discussed in 2.9 are an example of a formalism where both ordering and dependency are intended interpretations. As was the case for ordering and constituency with CFGs, interpretations in terms of ordering and dependency are not independent for simple DGs. Specifically, condition (18) holds for all structural descriptions generated by DGs (cf. Gaifman 1965: 306).

(18) If a structural description σ generated by a DG is assigned an interpretation $i_o \in \mathrm{ID_O}$ by $\mathrm{IF_{DG\rightarrow O}}$, $i_o = \{\langle x_i, i\rangle, 1 \leq i \leq n\}$, then, for every occurrence in σ, that occurrence and all those occurrences which depend on it indirectly form a continuous substring of the set of occurrences.

This property is known as *projectivity* in the dependency theory literature.[15] More generally, the following theorem holds:

(19) DGs are able to express all and only the pairs of interpretations in terms of dependency and order satisfying (17) and (18).

2.12 Constituent Structures Expressed by DGs

Consider the structural description in Figure 2.5 above. There are two obvious ways to interpret such structures as assigning a constituent structure to their terminal strings, beyond the central dependency interpretation. Both define as constituents those sets of occurrences comprising an occurrence and all of the occurrences that indirectly depend on it.[16] The second further defines all occurrences as forming

---

[15] See for instance Marcus 1967. What we are defining here as *projectivity* is what Gladkii (1970: 17ff) calls *strong projectivity*.

[16] Note that we implicitly made use of this constituency interpretation in our

singleton constituents.[17] Interpretation Functions for both these intuitions are given in (20) and (21) respectively.

(20) $IF_{DG \to C} : \Sigma(DG) \to ID_C: \sigma \to \Gamma$ such that $\forall B \in V_N, \{b \in V_T \mid b$ is a descendent of $B\} \in \Gamma$.

For the structure in Figure 2.5 , this gives us.

$\Gamma = \{\{\langle \text{the}, 1\rangle\}, \{\langle \text{her}, 5\rangle\}, \{\langle \text{the}, 1\rangle, \langle \text{girl}, 2\rangle\}, \{\langle \text{her}, 5\rangle, \langle \text{mother}, 6\rangle\}, \{\langle \text{to}, 4\rangle, \langle \text{her}, 5\rangle, \langle \text{mother}, 6\rangle\}, \{\langle \text{the}, 1\rangle, \langle \text{girl}, 2\rangle, \langle \text{spoke}, 3\rangle, \langle \text{to}, 4\rangle, \langle \text{her}, 5\rangle, \langle \text{mother}, 6\rangle\}\}$

(21) $IF_{DG \to C} : \Sigma(DG) \to ID_C: \sigma \to \Gamma$ such that:
(i) $\forall B \in V_N, \{b \in V_T \mid b$ is a descendent of $B\} \in \Gamma$; and
(ii) $\forall B \in V_N \mid B$ has at least one daughter belonging to V_N, the singleton $\{b \in V_T \mid b$ is a daughter of $B\} \in \Gamma$.

For the structure in Figure 2.5 , this gives us.

$\Gamma = \{\{\langle \text{the}, 1\rangle\}, \{\langle \text{girl}, 2\rangle\}, \{\langle \text{spoke}, 3\rangle\}, \{\langle \text{to}, 4\rangle\}, \{\langle \text{her}, 5\rangle\}, \{\langle \text{mother}, 6\rangle\}, \{\langle \text{the}, 1\rangle, \langle \text{girl}, 2\rangle\}, \{\langle \text{her}, 5\rangle, \langle \text{mother}, 6\rangle\}, \{\langle \text{to}, 4\rangle, \langle \text{her}, 5\rangle, \langle \text{mother}, 6\rangle\}, \{\langle \text{the}, 1\rangle, \langle \text{girl}, 2\rangle, \langle \text{spoke}, 3\rangle, \langle \text{to}, 4\rangle, \langle \text{her}, 5\rangle, \langle \text{mother}, 6\rangle\}\}$

In what follows, we will adopt definition (21) for $IF_{DG \to C}$. A few remarks are in order.

First, this is a further example of the importance of defining Interpretation Functions explicitly. We are forced to choose here between two legitimate and a priori equally plausible interpretations for constituency. Second, note that it is also possible to define an interpretation in terms of labeled constituency for DGs. The obvious idea is to assign to constituents the label of the node that dominates them. Finally, the set of constituent structures expressible by DGs is clearly much more restricted than that expressible by CFGs. More specifically, we have the following theorem, which, using the terminology to be introduced in Chapter 3, means that DGs are strictly included in SGC in CFGs with respect to constituency.

---

definitions of the relations c-dependency and head-of in 2.8.

[17] The idea of interpreting derivations in DGs in this way goes back to Gaifman (1965: 316), who adopts a definition equivalent to (21).

(22) a. For every DG G there is a CFG G' such that $IF_{DG\rightarrow C}(\Sigma(G)) = IF_{CFG\rightarrow C}(\Sigma(G'))$.
b. There are CFGs G' such that there is no DG G such that $IF_{DG\rightarrow C}(\Sigma(G)) = IF_{CFG\rightarrow C}(\Sigma(G'))$.

We can in fact define the subset of ID_C that can be specified by derivations in DGs (that is, the image of Σ(DG) by $IF_{DG\rightarrow C}$), namely it is that subset of ID_C containing all and only the constituent structures Γ on a set S of occurrences such that:[18]

(23) a. S belongs to Γ; and
b. If E_1 and E_2 belong to Γ, and the intersection of E_1 and E_2 is not empty, then :
E_1 is included in E_2; or
E_2 is included in E_1; and
c. For all E_i belonging to Γ, there is an E_j belonging to Γ such that (i) E_j is included in E_i; (ii) E_j is a singleton; (iii) there is no E_k in Γ such that E_j is strictly included in E_k and E_k is strictly included in E_i;
d. Every occurrence of S forms a singleton constituent of Γ.

Conditions (23a, b), which are also properties of the constituent structures defined by CFGs (cf. above 2.5.1), follow from (22a). (23c) is obvious, given the definition of terminated derivations in DGs, namely the fact that for a derivation to be terminated, every nonterminal must be rewritten as a terminal by a lexical rule. That terminal will form the singleton constituent directly included in the constituent dominated by the nonterminal. (23d) results from the choice made with respect to syncategorematic terminals in (21).

2.13 Interdependence of Constituency and Dependency Interpretations for DGs

DGs can produce structural descriptions defining any dependency relations satisfying conditions (17a, b) and (18) above on an arbitrary string. But, if a certain constituent structure is assigned to the string, this is no longer true in general. DGs cannot produce the whole cross-product of their possible interpretations in terms of dependency and their possible interpretations in terms of constituency. For instance, it is impossible to generate a structural description for a string *abcd* with a

---

[18] Proof of (23c) derives directly from Gaifman's theorem 3.8 (1965: 324).

DG such that *abcd* is assigned the constituent structure *[[ab][cd]]* and *a* and *b* both directly depend on *c*. These constraints will be discussed more specifically below in 4.1, and compared with the situation in phrase structure grammars.

2.14 Expressibility of Dependency by CFGs

Having shown that the structural descriptions generated by DGs allow an interpretation in terms of constituency, beyond their central dependency interpretation, the question arises as to whether derivations generated by CFGs allow a dependency interpretation in addition to their central constituency interpretation. This is an important question, especially in the light of the success of X-bar syntax, which is classically interpreted as assigning a head-of interpretation (and, as discussed above in 2.8, consequently also a dependency interpretation). For example, under the usual interpretation of headedness in X-bar grammars, the structure in Figure 2.6 expresses the dependency relation in (24a, b) and the head-of relation (24c).

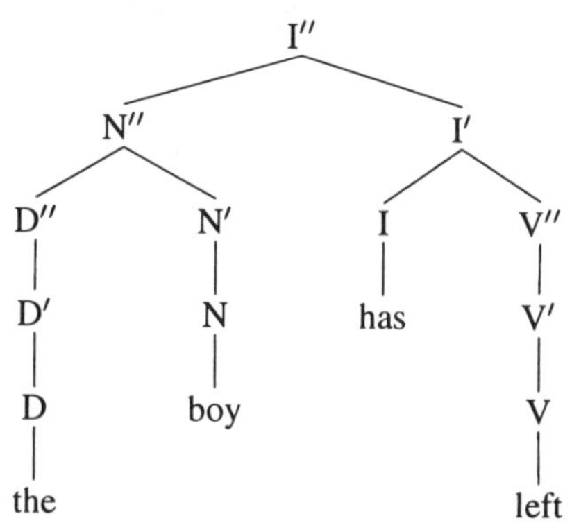

Figure 2.6

(24) a. 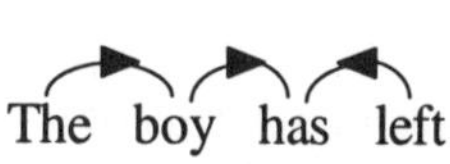

b. $R = \{\langle \text{the, boy} \rangle, \langle \text{boy, has} \rangle, \langle \text{left, has} \rangle\}$

c. $R' = \{\langle \text{the}, \{\text{the}\} \rangle, \langle \text{boy}, \{\text{the, boy}\} \rangle, \langle \text{left}, \{\text{left}\} \rangle,$
$\langle \text{has}, \{\text{the, boy, has, left}\} \rangle\}$

In order for us to understand the status of dependency relations on phrase structure grammars, it is necessary to discuss first the notion of what constitutes a legitimate interpretation for a formalism.

2.15 Legitimate Interpretation Functions

Up to this point, we have imposed no constraints on the nature of Interpretation Functions. This is a problem, in the sense that we want to be sure that Interpretation Functions cannot add information which is not in fact specified by the formalism (this would be a case of *overinterpreting* the formalism). The following definition of what constitutes a legitimate Interpretation Function guarantees that this will not occur.[19]

Definition*:* Legitimate Interpretation Function

> An Interpretation Function for a formalism is legitimate if and only if arbitrary relabeling of the vocabularies defined by the formalism preserves the results of the Interpretation Function.

This definition allows us to raise the following questions and to give them a relevant answer: (i) Are X-bar grammars CFGs? (ii) Do CFGs have a legitimate interpretation in terms of dependency?

In the light of the above definition, the answer to these questions is clear once one takes into account the fact that the bar marking in X-bar syntax is crucial to the dependency interpretation. Indeed, if one considers an X-bar grammar to be a CFG, then a label like X″ must be understood to be a fancy notation for an atomic symbol. This is because CFGs define a single vocabulary V_N of atomic categories for nonterminals. Obviously, an arbitrary relabeling of V_N will not, in general, preserve bar markings and the results of the Interpretation Function to dependency for X-bar grammars will not be preserved under such a relabeling, since it necessarily relies on bar marking information. Thus, it is clear that X-bar grammars cannot be taken to be simple CFGs, if their structural descriptions are to have an interpretation in terms of dependency. In order for the intended dependency interpretation for X-bar grammars to be a legitimate interpretation in terms of dependency, it is sufficient, for instance, to define them as involving n+1 nonterminal

[19] Note that for this definition to work as it is intended to, it is necessary to interpret the notion of preserving results as mapping to the same equivalence class in an Interpretation Domain, as discussed in the technical notes of 2.3 and 2.8.

vocabularies, where n is the highest bar level, or to define them as involving the rewriting of pairs $\langle X, n\rangle$, the first element belonging to the set of categories V_N and the second element belonging to the set of bar levels B, where both V_N and B are explicitly specified in the definition of the grammar.[20] As for question (ii), it is clear that CFGs allow no interpretation in terms of dependency that corresponds to the types of intuitions that we share about dependency. Indeed, whenever dependency interpretations for CFGs have been proposed, they have involved internal analysis of the node labels, either by assigning features of the bar type to elements of V_N or by considering the relations between node labels of the type NP and N as significant.[21] Note however that it is not simply impossible to assign a dependency interpretation to the trees generated by a CFG. It is easy, for instance to define a legitimate Interpretation Function such that all occurrences in the string depend on the first occurrence, or such that all occurrences depend on the leftmost of the most deeply embedded occurrences in the tree. However, such interpretations are totally unrelated to our intuitions about the expression of dependency by CFG related formalisms and can therefore be ignored.

This definition of legitimacy for Interpretation Functions allows us to understand the actual status of an interesting problem concerning the expressive power of type-0 grammars (unrestricted rewriting systems) that was raised by Manaster-Ramer 1987a and discussed by Pullum 1989. Manaster-Ramer claims that "as far as wgc goes, type-0 grammars are the most powerful generative devices there can be, but it is child's play to construct a tree set which is beyond their sgc (to the extent that sgc can be defined for these grammars" (Manaster-Ramer 1987a: 224). Manaster-Ramer specifically cites unbounded branching as something which can be done by a CFG augmented with the Kleene star, but not by a type-0 grammar. Pullum points out the paradoxical nature of Manaster-Ramer's statement ("If it is child's play to construct a set of trees that a type-0 grammar cannot generate, then type-0 grammars can hardly be 'the most powerful generative devices there can be'"). Pullum then goes on to show how a type-0 grammar, including labeled brackets (e.g. $[_{NP}, {}_{NP}]$) in its terminal vocabulary, can generate the

---

20 This is essentially the formalization of Bresnan 1976. The point made here shows, for instance, that the arguments in Williams 1981 to the effect that phrase names should not be analyzed as nonatomic cannot be interpreted as applying to bar-level, if one wants to preserve a legitimate dependency interpretation.

21 Cf. for instance the original proposals of Gaifman (1965: 319-20) which involve using a superscript w to distinguish head categories.

labeled bracketings corresponding to the unbounded branching tree structures generated by CFGs augmented with the Kleene star, thus apparently falsifying Manaster-Ramer's claim.

Given the framework set up in this chapter, it is clear that there is no genuine dispute going on here, because the terms of the debate have not been drawn up coherently. Manaster-Ramer is right that type-0 grammars as classically defined do not allow for unbounded branching, but he is right only for the trivial reason that they do not allow for a legitimate interpretation in terms of branching at all. Note in this respect Manaster-Ramer's hedge "to the extent that sgc can be defined for [type-0] grammars" (it is obvious from the context that by 'sgc' he means an interpretation in terms of constituent structure). Consequently, Pullum is correct too in the sense that, as he points out, in order to talk about whether or not type-0 grammars define unbounded branching, you have to show how they define any branching at all, and once you have done that, unbounded branching raises no further difficulties. The problem is that for Pullum's construction to have a legitimate interpretation in terms of constituency, it cannot be a classical type-0 grammar, since the constituency interpretation relies on recognizing some elements of the terminal vocabulary as left or right labeled brackets. Obviously, an arbitrary relabeling of V_T will not preserve this property, and the relevant bracketing of the strings will be lost. It is possible to define a variant of type-0 grammars, inspired from Pullum's construction, which does support his intended interpretation. This would clearly involve distinguishing four separate vocabularies, the V_N, the V_T, the $V_[$, and the $V_]$.[22]

Thus the issue of whether type-0 grammars can or cannot generate sets of trees with unbounded degree of branching is resolvable only given explicit definitions of the Interpretation Domain and Interpretation Function that is assumed. If the choice is made in a way that does not assign trees at all to the terminal strings generated by type-0 grammars, then Manaster-Ramer's claim is true, but only trivially so. Making the choice in a way that permits trees to be defined involves defining a new type of grammar — though one that is weakly equivalent to type-0 grammars. When that is done, Manaster-Ramer's claim is false of the

---

[22] Note that it is not clear how one could redefine type-0 grammars adding a constraint on the form of productions which would ensure that every string generated would comprise a consistent labeled bracketing, i.e. be isomorphic to a tree structure, and this without restricting the class of languages generated. Such a constraint does presumably exist, however.

new grammar type, as Pullum argues — except that Pullum was speaking in terms of unmodified type-0 grammars, and of those his claim is false. The moral here is that choices of Interpretation Domain and Interpretation Function must be explicitly made before comparison of this sort between different grammatical theories can be meaningfully discussed.

Before closing this chapter, which has introduced the spirit in which I will be discussing SGC in the rest of this study, it is necessary to comment on a central property of the analysis. Namely, the objects that we are considering to be relevant for the interpretation of a grammar or formalism are the structural descriptions specified by that grammar or formalism, rather than the definition of the grammar or formalism itself. It is impossible at this stage of the discussion to justify this position, but we will return to this property in 3.7.

Chapter 3

Strong Generative Capacity: the Semantics of Linguistic Formalism

Having set the stage in the preceding chapter, it is now time for us to provide a set of explicit definitions for SGC on which we will rely in the rest of this study. Recall that an *Interpretation Domain* is a set of abstract set-theoretic representations for a class of linguistically relevant properties of a formalism (or *theory*, I am using both of these terms synonymously here), and that an *Interpretation Function* $\mathrm{IF}_{\mathrm{B}\rightarrow\mathrm{A}}$ maps structural representations in formalism *B* to their intended interpretation in the Interpretation Domain ID_{A}. Thus, for each formalism, and for each Interpretation Domain which is relevant for that formalism, we need an Interpretation Function mapping the structural representations generated by grammars in that formalism into the Interpretation Domain.

3.1 SGC of a Grammar *G* with respect to an Interpretation Domain ID_i

The *SGC of a grammar G*, in a theory *T*, with respect to the Interpretation Domain ID_i is the image of $\Sigma(G)$ by the corresponding Interpretation Function $\mathrm{IF}_{\mathrm{T}\rightarrow\mathrm{i}}$ (i.e. it is the range of $\mathrm{IF}_{\mathrm{T}\rightarrow\mathrm{i}}$).[1]

$$\mathrm{SGC}_{\mathrm{ID}_i}(G) = \mathrm{IF}_{\mathrm{T}\rightarrow\mathrm{i}}(\Sigma(G))$$

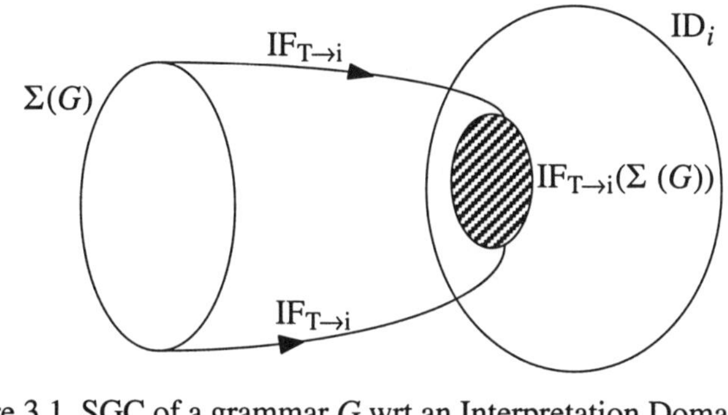

Figure 3.1. SGC of a grammar *G* wrt an Interpretation Domain ID_i

[1] Recall that $\Sigma(G)$ is defined as the set of structural descriptions specified by the grammar *G*.

3.2 SGC of a Theory T with respect to an Interpretation Domain ID_i

The *SGC of a theory T* which provides Grammars $\{G_1, G_2, ...\}$ with respect to the Interpretation Domain ID_i is the set $\{\mathrm{IF}_{\mathrm{T}\to\mathrm{i}}(\Sigma(G_1)), \mathrm{IF}_{\mathrm{T}\to\mathrm{i}}(\Sigma(G_2)), ...\}$ of images of the $\Sigma(G_k)$ by the corresponding Interpretation Function $\mathrm{IF}_{\mathrm{T}\to\mathrm{i}}$.

$$\mathrm{SGC}_{\mathrm{ID}_i}(T) = \{\mathrm{IF}_{\mathrm{T}\to\mathrm{i}}(\Sigma(G_1)), \mathrm{IF}_{\mathrm{T}\to\mathrm{i}}(\Sigma(G_2)), ...\}$$

Let us define $\Sigma(T)$ as $\Sigma(G_1) \cup \Sigma(G_2) \cup ...$, where T is a theory which provides the set of grammars $\{G_1, G_2, ...\}$. Then, $\mathrm{IF}_{\mathrm{T}\to\mathrm{i}}(\Sigma(T))$ is the set of interpretations that can be obtained for structural descriptions generated by any grammar provided by the theory T.

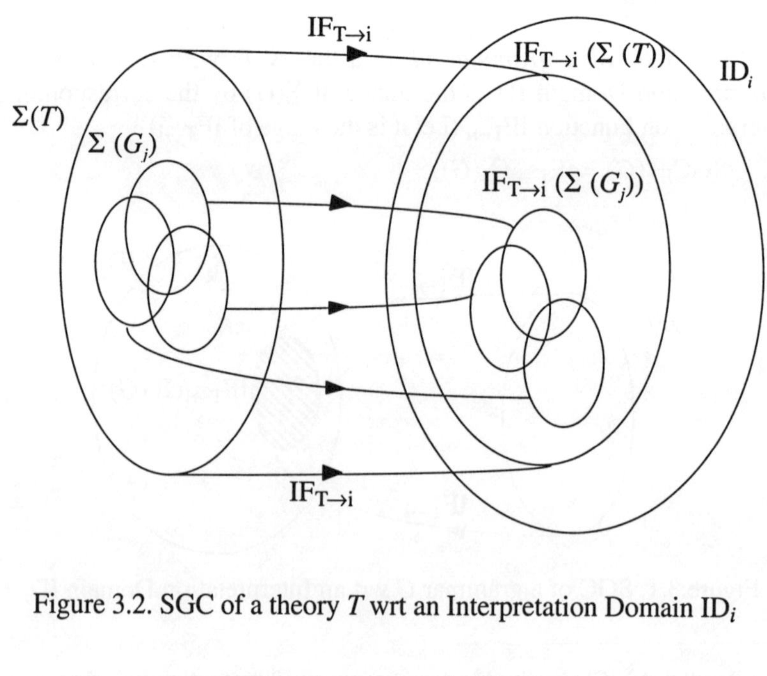

Figure 3.2. SGC of a theory T wrt an Interpretation Domain ID_i

It is important to note that we do not want to equate $\mathrm{IF}_{\mathrm{T}\to\mathrm{i}}(\Sigma(T))$ with SGC(T). SGC(T) as defined above specifies the information given by $\mathrm{IF}_{\mathrm{T}\to\mathrm{i}}(\Sigma(T))$, but furthermore tells us which subsets of $\mathrm{IF}_{\mathrm{T}\to\mathrm{i}}(\Sigma(T))$ can be represented by individual grammars provided by T. This is important information. For example, for every derivation σ which can be generated by a Context-Sensitive Grammar (CSG),[2] there is a derivation σ' generated by a CFG defining the same constituent structure as σ. Thus, $\mathrm{IF}_{\mathrm{CSG}\to\mathrm{LC}}(\Sigma(\mathrm{CSG})) = \mathrm{IF}_{\mathrm{CFG}\to\mathrm{LC}}(\Sigma(\mathrm{CFG}))$. Consequently, if we defined the SGC of T with respect to $\mathrm{ID}_{\mathrm{LC}}$ as $\mathrm{IF}_{\mathrm{T}\to\mathrm{LC}}(\Sigma(T))$, we would be saying that CFGs and CSGs have the same SGC with respect to labeled constituency. But we do not want to say this because we would lose the crucial fact that there are sets of labeled constituent structures which are specified by a single CSG but not by any single CFG. The same thing is true for Tree Adjoining Grammars (TAGs, cf. 3.8) and CFGs.

However, in some situations the notion expressed by $\mathrm{IF}_{\mathrm{T}\to\mathrm{i}}(\Sigma(T))$ is useful. We will refer to it as the *range of interpretations* expressed by the theory T with respect to the Interpretation Domain ID_i.

3.3 SGC of a Grammar G with respect to a Tuple of Interpretation Domains $\langle \mathrm{ID}_1, \ldots, \mathrm{ID}_n \rangle$

The SGC of a Grammar G, provided by a theory T, with respect to a tuple of Interpretation Domains $\langle \mathrm{ID}_1, \ldots, \mathrm{ID}_n \rangle$ is the set of tuples of interpretations in the Cartesian product of these Interpretation Domains such that for each tuple there is a structural description σ in G which is mapped to the tuple by the relevant Interpretation Functions.

$$\mathrm{SGC}_{\mathrm{ID}_1,\ldots,\mathrm{ID}_n}(G) = \{\langle i_1, \ldots, i_n \rangle \in \mathrm{ID}_1 \times \ldots \times \mathrm{ID}_n \mid \exists\sigma, \sigma \in \Sigma(G), \forall j, 1 \leq j \leq n, i_j = \mathrm{IF}_{\mathrm{T}\to\mathrm{j}}(\sigma)\}$$

---

2 CSGs are to be understood here as the type 2 grammars of Chomsky (1963: 363ff.), i.e. those that allow tree representations for their derivations.

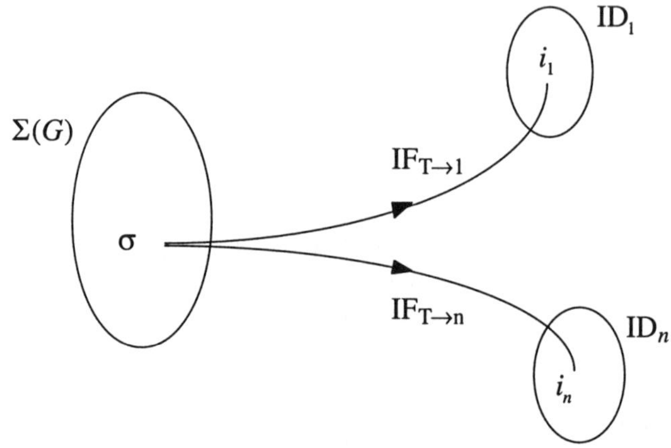

Figure 3.3. Mapping of a derivation in $\Sigma(G)$ to its interpretations in $\langle ID_1, ID_2, ..., ID_n \rangle$

Note that we do not want to define $SGC_{ID_1,...,ID_n}(G)$ as the tuple $\langle IF_{T\rightarrow 1}(\Sigma(G)), ..., IF_{T\rightarrow n}(\Sigma(G))\rangle$, because this is a much less informative concept. It will not account for the fact that, though all interpretations in all the sets $IF_{T\rightarrow 1}(\Sigma(G)), ..., IF_{T\rightarrow 1}(\Sigma(G))$ can be represented by structural descriptions specified by *G*, for a certain tuple of such interpretations there may be is no single structural description which maps to that tuple. We saw an instance of this in section 2.13 above, where we noted that among the dependency relations that can be defined on a string by a DG, only a subset will be compatible with any given choice of constituency for that string.

3.4 SGC of a Theory *T* with respect to a Tuple of Interpretation Domains $\langle ID_1, ..., ID_n \rangle$

The SGC of a Theory *T* providing grammars $\{G_1, G_2, ...\}$ with respect to a tuple of Interpretation Domains $\langle ID_1, ..., ID_n \rangle$ is the set $\{SGC_{ID_1,...,ID_n}(G_1), SGC_{ID_1,...,ID_n}(G_2), ...\}$ of SGCs of the grammars provided by *T*.

$$\mathrm{SGC}_{\mathrm{ID}_1,\ldots,\mathrm{ID}_n}(T) = \{\mathrm{SGC}_{\mathrm{ID}_1,\ldots,\mathrm{ID}_n}(G_1),\ \mathrm{SGC}_{\mathrm{ID}_1,\ldots,\mathrm{ID}_n}(G_2),\ \ldots\}$$

Note that instead of introducing the notion of SGC with respect to a tuple of Interpretation Domains $\langle \mathrm{ID}_1, \ldots, \mathrm{ID}_n \rangle$, we could just as easily have obtained a basically equivalent concept in terms of a single Interpretation Domain, by choosing this domain as the result of the Cartesian product of the *n* original Interpretation Domains. The reason for which we have not chosen this option is that it makes comparison of theories less perspicuous when the theories do not have the same sets of intended interpretations. For instance, if we analyzed the strong generative capacity of dependency grammars in terms of constituency and dependency using a single Interpretation Domain $\mathrm{ID}_{\mathrm{CD}} = \mathrm{ID}_{\mathrm{C}} \times \mathrm{ID}_{\mathrm{D}}$, this would make it difficult to compare the strong generative capacity of dependency grammars with that of context free grammars with respect to ID_{C}, the Interpretation Domain which they have in common as an intended interpretation.

3.5 Analogy with Model-theoretic Semantics

It should be noted that the above definitions are essentially identical to the way in which semantic interpretation is defined in model-theoretic semantics (cf. Montague 1974, Dowty et al. 1981). For a given theory *T*, we have a model $\langle A, F \rangle$ where *A* is the Cartesian product of the Interpretation Domains $\langle \mathrm{ID}_1, \ldots, \mathrm{ID}_n \rangle$ relevant for *T* ($A = \mathrm{ID}_1 \times \mathrm{ID}_2 \times \ldots \times \mathrm{ID}_n$) and *F* is the function which maps a structural description σ of *T* into tuples in *A*, such that $F(\sigma) = \langle \mathrm{IF}_{\mathrm{T}\rightarrow 1}(\sigma), \ldots, \mathrm{IF}_{\mathrm{T}\rightarrow n}(\sigma) \rangle$, where $\mathrm{IF}_{\mathrm{T}\rightarrow i}$ is the Interpretation Function mapping structural descriptions of *T* into ID_i. The only difference is that we are not interested here in the semantics of the sentences (i.e. their truth conditions, what they say about the world); instead we are interested in the semantics of the formalisms, that is, what linguistic properties a formalism attributes to an entity (sentence, word, etc.) by assigning to it a certain structural description. This is the sense in which our definition of SGC is a semantical one.

3.6 Comparing Grammars and Theories in SGC

3.6.1 Equivalence

3.6.1.1 Two Grammars G and G', provided by theories T and T', respectively, are *equivalent in SGC with respect to an Interpretation Domain ID* if and only if their images in ID by the relevant Interpretation Functions are identical.

$$\mathrm{SGC_{ID}}(G) = \mathrm{SGC_{ID}}(G') \text{ iff } \mathrm{IF_{T\to ID}}(\Sigma(G)) = \mathrm{IF_{T'\to ID}}(\Sigma(G'))$$

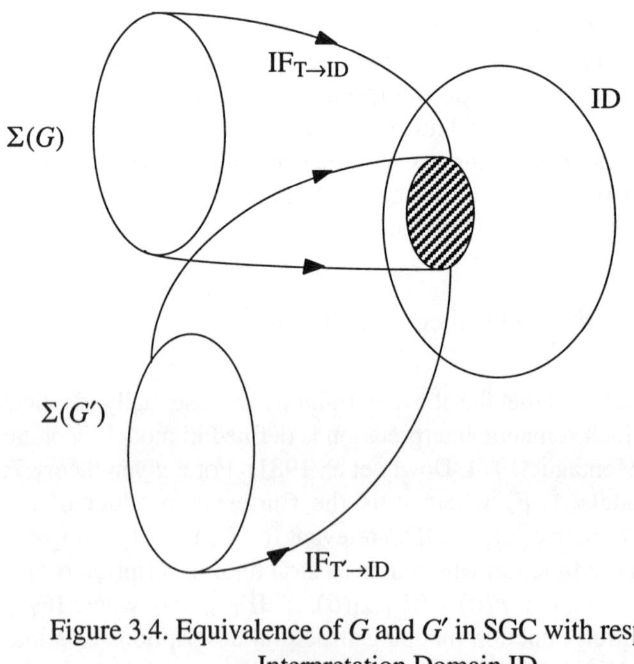

Figure 3.4. Equivalence of G and G' in SGC with respect to the Interpretation Domain ID

This definition can also be expressed in the following equivalent way:

Two Grammars G and G', provided by theories T and T' respectively, are *equivalent in SGC with respect to an Interpretation Domain ID* iff there are mappings $\phi : \Sigma(G) \to \Sigma(G')$ and $\phi' : \Sigma(G') \to \Sigma(G)$ such that

(i) $\forall \sigma_1 \in \Sigma(G), \exists \sigma_2 \in \Sigma(G') \mid \sigma_2 = \phi(\sigma_1)$ and $\mathrm{IF_{T\to ID}}(\sigma_1) = \mathrm{IF_{T'\to ID}}(\sigma_2)$; and

(ii) $\forall \sigma_2 \in \Sigma(G'), \exists \sigma_1 \in \Sigma(G) \mid \sigma_1 = \phi'(\sigma_2)$ and $\mathrm{IF_{T\to ID}}(\sigma_1) = \mathrm{IF_{T'\to ID}}(\sigma_2)$

The latter definition is useful in constructing proofs of equivalence, and furthermore can be extended to provide a simple definition of equivalence of grammars with respect to a tuple of Interpretation Domains.[3]

3.6.1.2 Two Grammars G and G', provided by theories T and T' respectively, are *equivalent in SGC with respect to a tuple of Interpretation Domains* $\langle \mathrm{ID}_1, ..., \mathrm{ID}_n \rangle$ if and only if there are mappings $\phi : \Sigma(G) \rightarrow \Sigma(G')$ and $\phi' : \Sigma(G') \rightarrow \Sigma(G)$ such that

(i) $\forall \sigma_1 \in \Sigma(G), \exists \sigma_2 \in \Sigma(G') \mid \sigma_2 = \phi(\sigma_1)$ and $\forall i,\ 1 \leq i \leq n$, $\mathrm{IF}_{\mathrm{T}\rightarrow\mathrm{i}}(\sigma_1) = \mathrm{IF}_{\mathrm{T'}\rightarrow\mathrm{i}}(\sigma_2)$; and

(ii) $\forall \sigma_2 \in \Sigma(G'), \exists \sigma_1 \in \Sigma(G) \mid \sigma_1 = \phi'(\sigma_2)$ and $\forall i,\ 1 \leq i \leq n$, $\mathrm{IF}_{\mathrm{T}\rightarrow\mathrm{i}}(\sigma_1) = \mathrm{IF}_{\mathrm{T'}\rightarrow\mathrm{i}}(\sigma_2)$

This is illustrated in figure 5 on the following page.

It should be noted that two grammars that are equivalent with respect to an Interpretation Domain ID_1 and with respect to a second Interpretation Domain ID_2 are not necessarily equivalent with respect to the pair $\langle \mathrm{ID}_1, \mathrm{ID}_2 \rangle$. The latter is in fact a much stronger property. Indeed it requires that for every derivation in the derivation set of one grammar, which is mapped to a given pair of interpretations, there be a corresponding derivation in the derivation set of the other grammar expressing the same pair of interpretations, and vice versa. Two grammars can be equivalent with respect to ID_1 and with respect to ID_2 without this being the case.

---

[3] It is not possible to define equivalence between grammars on the basis of a bijective mapping between the sets of structural descriptions that they generate (e.g. two grammars G and G', provided by theories T and T' respectively, are equivalent in SGC with respect to an Interpretation Domain ID iff there is a bijective mapping ϕ from $\Sigma(G)$ to $\Sigma(G')$ such that if $\phi(\sigma_1) = (\sigma_2)$, $\sigma_1 \in \Sigma(G)$ and $\sigma_2 \in \Sigma(G')$, then $\mathrm{IF}_{\mathrm{T}\rightarrow\mathrm{i}}(\sigma_1) = \mathrm{IF}_{\mathrm{T'}\rightarrow\mathrm{i}}(\sigma_2)$). This is because there can be multiple structural descriptions generated by one of the grammars that have the same interpretation with respect to ID but only one structural description generated by the other grammar which has that same interpretation. In such cases, we still want to say that the grammars are equivalent with respect to ID if the conditions given in the text hold. Cases of this type will appear in the next chapter.

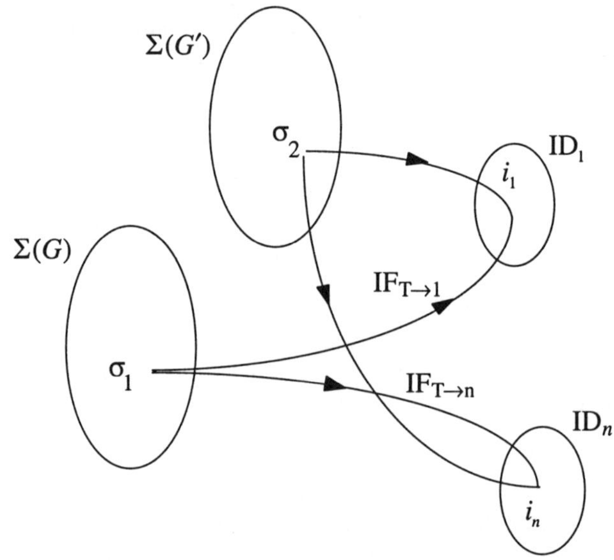

Figure 3.5. Equivalence of G and G' in SGC wrt a tuple $\langle \mathrm{ID}_1, ..., \mathrm{ID}_n \rangle$

3.6.1.3 Two Theories T, providing grammars $\{G_1, G_2, ...\}$, and T', providing grammars $\{G_1', G_2', ...\}$, *are equivalent in SGC with respect to a tuple of Interpretation Domains* $\langle \mathrm{ID}_1, ..., \mathrm{ID}_n \rangle$ iff there are mappings $\theta_1 : T \rightarrow T'$ and $\theta_2 : T' \rightarrow T$ such that

(i) $\forall G \in T, \exists G' \in T' \mid \theta_1(G) = G'$ and G and G' are equivalent in SGC with respect to $\langle \mathrm{ID}_1, ..., \mathrm{ID}_n \rangle$; and

(ii) $\forall G' \in T', \exists G \in T \mid \theta_2(G') = G$ and G and G' are equivalent in SGC with respect to $\langle \mathrm{ID}_1, ..., \mathrm{ID}_n \rangle$.

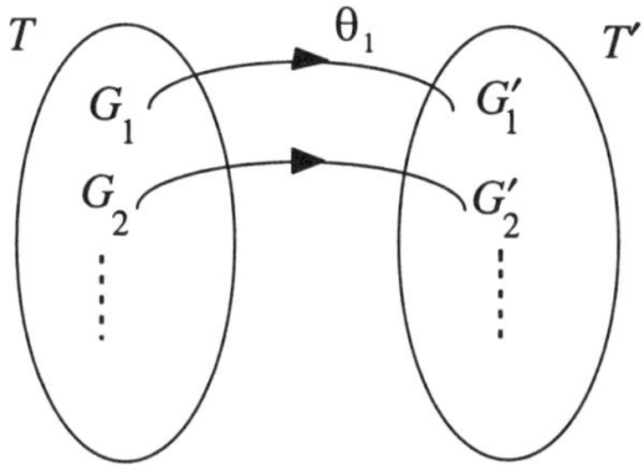

Figure 3.6. Equivalence of two theories T and T'

3.6.1.4 Two Theories T, providing grammars $\{G_1, G_2, ...\}$, and T', providing grammars $\{G_1', G_2', ...\}$, express *the same range of interpretations* with respect to a tuple of Interpretation Domains $\langle ID_1, ..., ID_n\rangle$ iff there are mappings $\phi : \Sigma(T) \rightarrow \Sigma(T')$ and $\phi' : \Sigma(T') \rightarrow \Sigma(T)$ such that

(i) $\forall \sigma_1 \in \Sigma(T), \exists \sigma_2 \in \Sigma(T') \mid \sigma_2 = \phi(\sigma_1)$ and $\forall i,\ 1 \leq i \leq n$, $IF_{T\rightarrow i}(\sigma_1) = IF_{T'\rightarrow i}(\sigma_2)$; and

(ii) $\forall \sigma_2 \in \Sigma(T'), \exists \sigma_1 \in \Sigma(T) \mid \sigma_1 = \phi'(\sigma_2)$ and $\forall i,\ 1 \leq i \leq n$, $IF_{T\rightarrow i}(\sigma_1) = IF_{T'\rightarrow i}(\sigma_2)$

This definition is exactly parallel to that given in 3.6.1.2. for the equivalence of grammars in SGC, with respect to tuples of Interpretation Domains, except that it establishes mappings between the derivations in $\Sigma(T)$ and $\Sigma(T')$.

3.6.2 Inclusion[4]

3.6.2.1 Grammar G, provided by Theory T, is *included in SGC* in Grammar G', provided by theory T', with respect to the tuple of Interpretation Domains $\langle ID_1, ..., ID_n\rangle$ iff either

(a) there is an mapping $\phi : \Sigma(G) \rightarrow \Sigma(G')$ such that $\forall \sigma_1 \in \Sigma(G), \exists \sigma_2 \in \Sigma(G') \mid \sigma_2 = \phi(\sigma_1)$ and $\forall i, 1 \leq i \leq n$, $IF_{T\rightarrow i}(\sigma_1) = IF_{T'\rightarrow i}(\sigma_2)$; or
(b) G and G' are equivalent wrt a tuple of Interpretation Domains $\langle ID_k, ID_{k'}, ...\rangle$, where $\{ID_k, ID_{k'}, ...\}$ is a subset of $\{ID_1, ..., ID_n\}$, and the

---

[4] It should be noted that in the case of inclusion in SGC for grammars and theories, various reasonable definitions other than the ones chosen here are possible.

remaining Interpretation Domains are not relevant for T, i.e. there are no Interpretation Functions mapping structural descriptions in T to those Interpretation Domains.

In case (a), we require that for every structural description in $\Sigma(G)$ there is an equivalent structural description in $\Sigma(G')$ but not necessarily vice versa. For strict inclusion we simply require that there be structural descriptions in $\Sigma(G')$ for which there is no equivalent structural description in $\Sigma(G)$.

Case (b) corresponds to a situation where for a given tuple of Interpretation Domains, theories T and T', in which grammars G and G' are respectively cast, share some of these Interpretation Domains but there are others which are only relevant for T'. Furthermore, with respect to the domains that are shared, G and G' are equivalent in SGC. The existence of Domains that are relevant for G' but not for G is interpreted as indicating a more restricted SGC for the latter.

3.6.2.2 Theory T, providing grammars $\{G_1, G_2, ...\}$, is *included in SGC* in Theory T', providing grammars $\{G_1', G_2', ...\}$, with respect to a tuple of Interpretation Domains $\langle ID_1, ..., ID_n\rangle$ iff either

(a) there is a mapping $\theta_1 : T \rightarrow T'$ such that $\forall G \in T, \exists G' \in T' \mid \theta_1(G) = G'$ and G and G' are equivalent in SGC wrt $\langle ID_1, ..., ID_n\rangle$; or

(b) There are mappings $\theta_1 : T \rightarrow T'$ and $\theta_2 : T' \rightarrow T$ such that

(i) $\forall G \in T, \exists G' \in T' \mid \theta_1(G) = G'$ and G is included in G' in SGC wrt $\langle ID_1, ..., ID_n\rangle$; and

(ii) $\forall G' \in T', \exists G \in T \mid \theta_2(G') = G$ and G is included in G' in SGC wrt $\langle ID_1, ..., ID_n\rangle$.

In case (a), theory T' may include grammars for which there is no corresponding grammar in T. In case (b), grammars in T are systematically included in SGC in the corresponding grammars in T'.

3.6.2.3 It is easy to define the idea that the range of interpretations expressed by a theory T with respect to a tuple of Interpretation Domains is included in the range of interpretations expressed by a theory T'. This can be done in a way exactly parallel to that used in 3.6.2.1. above for the case of grammars.

3.7 Interpreting Sets of Structural Descriptions vs. Interpreting Grammars: Ordering in ID/LP Grammars vs. Classical CFGs

One of the tenets of the theory of SGC proposed here is that it is the structural descriptions specified by grammars that are to be interpreted, rather than the grammars themselves. This position may seem counterintuitive, but I am going to argue here that it is not only tenable, but necessary if one wants to be able to compare grammars written in different formalisms. For this purpose, I will use the example of ordering constraints in classical CFGs and ID/LP grammars, examining at which level the difference between them should be established.

In classical CFGs, ordering properties of constituents are specified in tandem with their dominance properties by the context-free productions. Gazdar et al.1985 (henceforth GKPS), following Gazdar and Pullum 1981, propose to separate the statement of these two types of information, using what they call ID/LP grammars. Productions are defined to be Immediate Dominance (ID) rules, i.e. rules that specify the categories that can be daughters of a given category, without constraining the ordering between them. For instance, the ID rule $A \rightarrow B, C, D$ specifies that A may dominate nodes labeled B, C and D, but specifies no ordering among them (in order to distinguish them from ordinary context-free productions, ID rules are written with commas between the categories on the right hand side).

Ordering, on the other hand, is defined by Linear Precedence (LP) rules of the form $A \prec B$. Inclusion of such a rule in a grammar requires that, among sister nodes, a sister labeled A must precede a sister labeled B.[5] The LP rules of an ID/LP grammar specify an antisymmetric and transitive partial ordering over category labels.[6] This ordering defines a strict (irreflexive) ordering on multisets of sister nodes. Note that this

---

[5] More specifically, ordering among sister nodes is constrained by the transitive closure of the LP rules, i.e. if a grammar has LP rules $B \prec C$ and $C \prec D$, and B and D are sisters in a local tree, B must precede D, even in the absence of a sister labeled C in the same local tree.

[6] The partial ordering in question can be reflexive, irreflexive or non-reflexive, depending on the specific choice of LP rules. Since $A \prec B$ is interpreted as excluding daughter sequences with a B to the left of an A, there is no way for two sisters labeled A to comply with an LP statement of the type $A \prec A$; such an LP rule is legal, but its effect is to make it impossible for two nodes to occur as sisters if they are both of category A.

ordering of sister nodes is independent of the category of the mother node. As pointed out by GKPS, this property makes ID/LP grammars more restrictive than classical CFGs. It is impossible, for instance, to simulate, without relabeling, a CFG with rules $C \rightarrow A\ B$ and $D \rightarrow B\ A$ and without rules $C \rightarrow B\ A$ and $D \rightarrow A\ B$, since in such a grammar the ordering of A and B as sisters depends on the category of the mother. GKPS call this constraint on ID/LP grammars the Exhaustive Constant Partial Ordering Constraint (ECPO). It is theoretically interesting in this context to discuss how the analysis of SGC presented here is able to account for the specific ordering properties of ID/LP grammars, and ECPO in particular, in contrast with those of classical CFGs.

The fact that we are interpreting structural descriptions, rather than grammars means that we cannot directly interpret an LP rule $A \prec B$ to obtain a general statement about ordering and labeling properties of constituents in our grammars. Surely, however, this information is part of the intended semantics of the formalism, and should be captured by a theory of SGC. As it turns out, this is in fact easy to do.

Consider an ID/LP grammar G with the LP rule $A \prec B$. The derivation set $\Sigma(G)$ of G has $\mathrm{IF}_{\mathrm{ID/LP}\rightarrow\mathrm{OLC}}(\Sigma(G))$ as its image in $\mathrm{ID}_{\mathrm{OLC}}$, the Interpretation Domain for ordered labeled constituency. It is an obvious property of $\mathrm{IF}_{\mathrm{ID/LP}\rightarrow\mathrm{OLC}}(\Sigma(G))$ that it expresses the ordering generalization enforced by the LP rule $A \prec B$. It does so in the following sense: all of the ordered constituent structures in $\mathrm{IF}_{\mathrm{ID/LP}\rightarrow\mathrm{OLC}}(\Sigma(G))$ are such that if they contain two sister constituents labeled A and B, all of the occurrences in the constituent labeled A precede all of those in the constituent labeled B. A consequence of this way of looking at things is that a classical CFG, which by the nature of its rule set enforces the same ordering restriction, will be considered to express the same ordering generalization. For instance, the ID/LP grammar G with rule sets $ID = \{S \rightarrow (S), A, B; A \rightarrow a; B \rightarrow b\}$, $\mathrm{LP} = \{A \prec B\}$ and CFG G' with rule set $P = \{S \rightarrow (S)\ A\ B, A \rightarrow a, B \rightarrow b\}$ will have the same image in $\mathrm{ID}_{\mathrm{OLC}}$, and consequently will be strongly equivalent with respect to constituency, labeling and ordering. It might appear that this is an inappropriate way of looking at things, and that one should distinguish these two grammars in SGC because one of them directly characterizes the ordering generalization by a specific rule, whereas the other does so only indirectly. I would like to maintain that such a point of view is ultimately untenable because it precludes any comparison of grammars written in different formalisms. Granted, we must have the means to characterize the difference between ID/LP grammars and classical CFGs, but the level of rule systems is not the right one at which to do it.

In fact, the difference between ID/LP grammars and classical CFGs is easy to characterize within the system set up here. The natural place for establishing this distinction is at the level of the SGCs of the two formalisms themselves. Indeed it is easy to see that the theory of ID/LP grammars is strictly strongly included in the theory of classical CFGs with respect to ordered labeled constituency, and that the additional constraints weighing on ID/LP grammars precisely express the intended interpretation in terms of ordering of that formalism, namely the ECPO constraint. Specifically, for any ID/LP grammar G, $\mathrm{IF}_{\mathrm{ID/LP}\rightarrow\mathrm{OLC}}(\Sigma(G))$ necessarily has the following property, contrary to classical CFGs.

(1) If there is an i in $\mathrm{IF}_{\mathrm{ID/LP}\rightarrow\mathrm{OLC}}(\Sigma(G))$, such that in i there are two sister constituents labeled A and B and the occurrences in A precede those in B, then, either

(i) for all i' in $\mathrm{IF}_{\mathrm{ID/LP}\rightarrow\mathrm{OLC}}(\Sigma(G))$ such that there are two sister constituents in i' labeled A and B the occurrences in A precede those in B; or

(ii) for all i' in $\mathrm{IF}_{\mathrm{ID/LP}\rightarrow\mathrm{OLC}}(\Sigma(G))$ such that there are two sister constituents in i' labeled A and B and such that the occurrences in A precede those in B there is an i'' in $\mathrm{IF}_{\mathrm{ID/LP}\rightarrow\mathrm{OLC}}(\Sigma(G))$ identical to i' except that the occurrences dominated by B precede those dominated by A.

This property is the reflex of the fact that in the tree set of an ID/LP grammar, if A and B are sister nodes and A precedes B, then, either whenever A and B are sisters in any tree, A will precede B (this is the case where $A \prec B$ is an LP rule of the grammar), or there will be another tree identical to the first except that B precedes A (this is the case where the order between A and B is not constrained by the LP rules).

I want to argue that this is precisely the level at which the distinction in SGC between CFGs and ID/LP grammars *should* be established. To start with, it is obvious that we will not be able to do away with interpreting derivation sets in order to compare grammars and theories in SGC. Consequently, if we can avoid the additional requirement of interpreting rules directly, we should do so for simplicity. More importantly, it is completely unclear what the Interpretation Domains for rules of grammars should be. And it is even less clear how such Interpretation Domains could be construed so that rules from different formalism could be interpreted into the same domains, and relevantly compared. All the more so that there is not necessarily a one-to-one mapping between rule sets of grammars which we would want to consider equivalent, but which are written in different formalisms (consider simply a variant of CFGs that separates the expression of dominance and ordering but allows as rich a theory of ordering as CFGs). The idea of interpreting grammars directly, by interpretation of their rule sets thus clearly leads back to the dilemma of incommensurability of SGC between different formalisms. The only way to avoid this problem is to study what grammars say about sentences by assigning them a given structural description. This is possible because we can assume that different styles of grammars can sometimes say similar things about sentences, even if the mechanisms that they use to express them are totally unrelated and incomparable. Thus, the crucial advantage of placing ourselves at the level of the structural descriptions generated by the grammars is that it allows us to ignore the irrelevant differences in the ways the rules of grammars are expressed, but to capture the relevant similarities and differences in what those grammars state about the sentences they generate.

To conclude this discussion, returning to the concrete example at hand, I claim that the theory of SGC presented here is correct in claiming that an ID/LP grammar and a classical CFG can be equivalent in SGC with respect to ordered labeled constituency, even though the ordering properties of constituents are directly stated in one, but not in the other. On the other hand, the SGC of the class of ID/LP grammars as a whole is strictly included in that of the classical CFGs. The advantage of our theory of SGC is precisely that it allows us to overcome superficial and irrelevant distinctions between grammar formats, such as whether a constraint is stated directly or indirectly, and to correctly characterize the relevant differences and similarities.

3.8 What is a Structural Description?

In this study, I am defining structural descriptions as those objects specified by grammars of a theory, which contain all the necessary information required for the Interpretation Functions for that theory to be able to interpret them. Given our definition of legitimacy for Interpretation Functions (cf. 2.15), this imposes strong conditions on the form of structural descriptions. I will discuss two examples, the relevant structural descriptions in Tree Adjoining Grammars (TAGs), and the configurational definition of grammatical relations in Chomsky 1965.

3.8.1 Structural Descriptions in TAGs

TAG is a tree generating system (see e.g. Joshi 1985, 1987, Joshi and Schabes 1997, Vijay-Shanker 1987, Weir 1988, Rambow 1994; I will be discussing only the most elementary TAG formalism in this section). It consists of a finite set of elementary trees and a composition operation (adjoining) which builds derived trees out of elementary trees and derived trees by adjoining. More technically, a TAG can be defined as a quadruple $\langle I, A, V_N, V_T \rangle$, where I and A are finite sets of elementary trees over V_N and V_T, respectively initial trees and auxiliary trees. In an initial tree, all leaves are terminals. In an auxiliary tree, all leaves but one are terminals, and one leaf is labeled with the same terminal as the root of the tree. Initial and auxiliary trees are illustrated in Figures 3.7 and 3.8 respectively, and the adjunction of an auxiliary tree into another tree is illustrated in Figure 3.9 (the Figures are taken from Joshi 1987: 88, 89, 108).

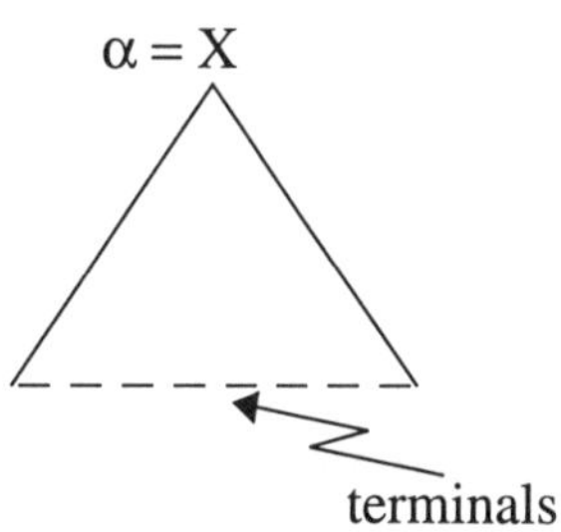

Figure 3.7

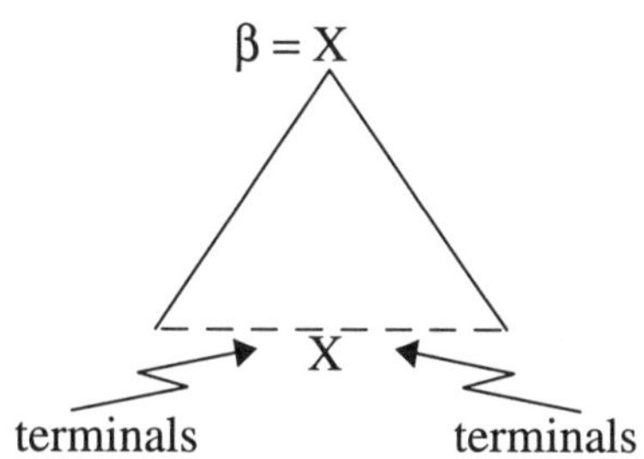

Figure 3.8

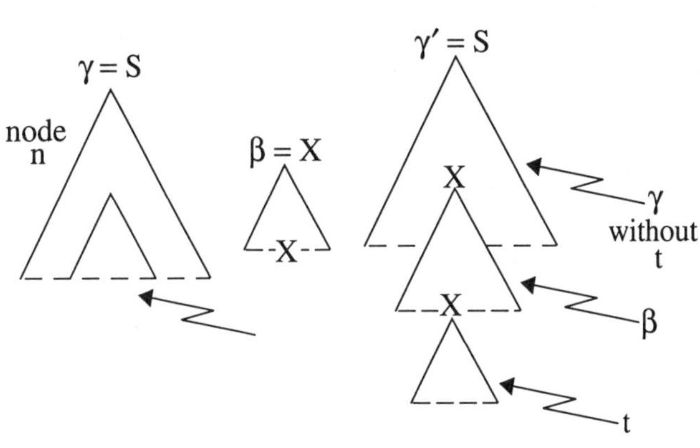

Figure 3.9

Users of TAGs have distinguished the 'derived trees', resulting from operations like the one illustrated in Figure 3.9, and which indicate the constituent structure and terminal string of a sentence, from the more abstract notion of 'derivation trees', illustrated in Figure 3.10. These indicate how a derived tree is obtained in the grammar by showing which elementary trees are adjoined into each other and at which node addresses[7] adjunction takes place.

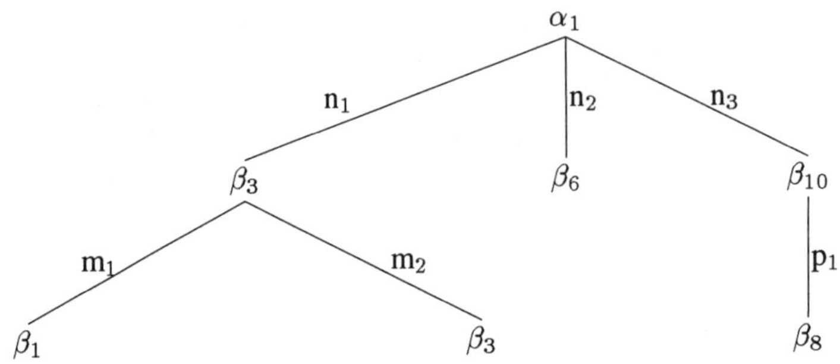

Figure 3.10

For instance, in figure 10, (a) auxiliary trees β_1 and β_3 are respectively adjoined at addresses m_1 and m_2 in auxiliary tree β_3; (b) auxiliary tree β_8 is adjoined at address p_1 in auxiliary tree β_{10}; (c) the results of (a), (b), and auxiliary tree β_6 are adjoined at addresses n_1, n_3 and n_2 respectively in the initial tree α_1.

Consequently, a derivation tree gives access to all of the information in the corresponding derived tree, but not vice-versa, since a given derived tree may be ambiguous between different derivations (differing either in loci of adjunction, or even in the elementary trees involved).

We thus see that if simple TAGs are to allow legitimate interpretations in terms of the notion of elementary sentential unit (what Rambow, Niv and Becker 1992 have called *derivational generative capacity* cf. chapter 7), their structural descriptions must be the derivation trees, not the derived trees.

---

[7] Cf. below 6.1.1 for discussion of this notion.

3.8.2 The Configurational Definition of Grammatical Relations

Similarly, consider the implications of our criterion of legitimacy for Interpretation Functions with respect to the definition of structural descriptions in a theory like that proposed in Chomsky 1965, which relies on a configurational definition of grammatical relations. The status of a rule which says 'the NP directly dominated by S is the subject of S' must be understood as a rule of the grammar, which crucially adds information to the structural description of the sentence. Otherwise, there is no legitimate Interpretation Function for the notion Subject-of. Note in this regard that the following Interpretation Function is illegitimate, where ID_{Rel} is the interpretation domain for grammatical relations.

(2) $IF_{CFG \rightarrow Rel}$: $\Sigma(CFG) \rightarrow ID_{Rel}$: $\sigma \rightarrow$ Rel such that if a constituent C_1 labeled NP in σ is directly dominated by a constituent C_2 labeled S, then SUBJ(C_1, C_2) is in Rel, and ... (where '...' defines the other desired relations on σ).

Indeed, arbitrary relabeling of V_N will not preserve the results of such an Interpretation Function. In order to get a legitimate interpretation in terms of grammatical relations, we need to enrich the notion of structural description defined by the grammar so that the information is present in the structural description independently of the constituent labeling by V_N, and can consequently be legitimately interpreted. This can be done by taking a rule similar to the illegitimate Interpretation Function just given as a rule of the grammar, which adds information to the structural description (e.g. one could add an LFG-style notation of the form ($\uparrow$SUBJ = $\downarrow$) to the NP node).

The reason for which this is the right way of thinking of these things should be obvious. If grammatical relations are an intended property of sentences, then they should be expressed by the grammars that generate the sentences, i.e. they should have their place *in* the formalism. This is not the case if they are expressed by the Interpretation Functions, the role of which is to interpret what representations in a formalism say, not to say things in their place. A notion like 'subject' is part of a theory of grammar, not just part of its interpretation.

Note that the point being made here depends on the assumption that relabeling of vocabularies is not accompanied by simultaneous relabeling of the Interpretation Functions. But it is crucially necessary to forbid such relabeling of the statement of Interpretation Functions in order to ensure that they cannot add information not provided by the theory to the derivations. Otherwise we lose the distinction between the content of the theory and its interpretation: the Interpretation Function becomes part of the theory.

Finally, it should be noted that in this study I am using the terms structural description and derivation as synonyms, though there might be reasons to reserve the latter for its more classical sense in formal language theory, where it pertains to the definition of WGC, and is not intended to support any properties related to SGC of the type just discussed.

3.9 Conclusion

We have introduced a semantically oriented conception of SGC. The advantages of this method are obvious. First, rather than staying at the level of the structures produced by a formalism, we are getting a handle on what the formalism is claiming about the sentences (or other linguistic structures) specified by assigning them certain structures. We are providing an analysis of what the structural descriptions express, and more generally, giving an analysis of the expressive power of the formalisms in terms independent of the formalisms themselves. In effect, we are providing a model-theoretic semantic interpretation for the descriptions produced by grammatical formalisms. Second, as a consequence of this last fact, it becomes possible to compare formalisms using crucially different types of structural descriptions, since we are no longer comparing the form of the descriptions, but their expressive content. We have consequently overcome the incommensurability problem pointed out by Rounds, Manaster-Ramer and Friedman 1987, and discussed at the end of chapter 1. Third, the method proposed gives us a way of deciding whether a certain interpretation can be legitimately attributed to a given formalism: an interpretation is legitimate for a formalism only if it is preserved under relabeling of the vocabularies of the formalism.

It should be noted that the proposed understanding of SGC is crucially intentional and relativistic. Namely, it is intentional in the sense that it crucially relies on the idea that an interpretation is relevant for purposes of SGC only if it is intended by the user of the formalism. Furthermore, the specific choice of an Interpretation Function, from the structures produced in a given formalism into a given Interpretation Domain, can only be justified on the basis of the intentions of the users of the formalism. It is relativistic in the sense that it does not allow one to simply say that two formalisms are equivalent in SGC. One can only say that they are equivalent with respect to a given set of Interpretation Domains, and a given choice of Interpretation Functions. In this sense, we have succeeded in providing a notion of equivalence of structural description (and more generally, equivalence in SGC), which is "attuned to the tolerance of our intuitions toward syntactic structures", thus satisfying Levelt's requirements discussed in chapter 1. Note however that the techniques presented here do impose a crucial limit on the liberty of choice of intended interpretations by the users of a formalism, by giving a criterion for legitimate interpretations.

Finally, I would like to point out the heuristic value of this technique of analysis of SGC, and that at two levels. First, by making it necessary to specify explicit Interpretation Domains, it forces one to think about the precise nature of the specific linguistic properties that one is trying to capture: what is it that one is trying to say about the linguistic units under analysis, be they sentences, phrases or words? This can lead to clarification, new distinctions, and new ideas in general. Second, by making it necessary to specify explicit Interpretation Functions, this analysis of SGC forces us to think about what properties we attribute to sentences (or other linguistic entities) by assigning them a given structure. In case we are not satisfied with the results, we may either redefine the formalism (e.g. one could redefine CFGs, so as to forbid syncategorematic terminals, if one refuses the idea of unlabeled constituents, or of occurrences that are not constituents), or we may redefine the Interpretation Functions themselves in a more appropriate way.

Chapter 4

Constituency, Dependency, Ordering, and Endocentricity in Phrase Structure Grammars

In this chapter, I will consider a number of variants of classical CFGs and discuss their SGC with respect to constituency, dependency, endocentricity and ordering. A first set of variants, including Marked Context-Free Grammars (MCFGs), Weakly Marked Context-Free Grammars (WMCFGs), Strongly Marked Context-Free Grammars (SMCFGs) and X-Bar Grammars (XBGs) are designed to support interpretations in terms of dependency. They will be discussed in section 4.1. Section 4.2. analyzes the expressive power of a second set of formalisms, including Liberation Grammars (LGs), Transformational Grammars with reordering transformations (TGs), and ID/PLP grammars, which are designed to support various types of discontinuous constituency interpretations. Finally, section 4.3 provides a discussion of endocentricity interpretations (head-adjunct relations) in phrase structure based frameworks.

4.1 Phrase Structure Grammars and Dependency

4.1.1 Marked Context Free Grammars (MCFGs)

An MCFG is a 5-tuple $G = \langle V_N, V_T, \langle S, 1\rangle, 2, P\rangle$, similar to a CFG except that:[1]

- Nodes are labeled with pairs, the first member of which is an element of V_N, and the second an element of $\{0, 1\}$ (we henceforth note this set '2'). Nodes (and the constituents associated with them) labeled with a pair of the type $\langle A, 1\rangle$ and $\langle A, 0\rangle$ are said to be *marked* and *unmarked* respectively. We will refer to the sets of marked and unmarked pairs as V_N' and V_N° respectively.
- The initial symbol $\langle S, 0\rangle$ belongs to V_N°.
- Productions P rewrite elements of V_N as strings of pairs in $V_N' \cup V_N^{\circ}$ or as terminals, i.e. for a node labeled with a given pair $\langle A, n\rangle$ only the first element of the pair constrains which daughters can be attached to it; it can be rewritten independently of its marked or unmarked status. Productions are subject to the constraint in (1):

(1) $\forall p \in P$, either

a. $p = A \rightarrow B_1 \ldots B_n \mid A \in V_N, B_1, \ldots, B_n \in V_N' \cup V_N^{\circ}$ and $\exists! i \mid B_i \in V_N'$; or

b. $p = A \rightarrow a \mid A \in V_N$ and $a \in V_T$.

That is, (a) there is one and only one marked daughter in any mother-daughter configuration; (b) there are no syncategorematic terminals.[2]

For simplicity, we adopt the notational convention that elements of V_N' are noted as uppercase roman letters with a prime (e.g. $\langle A, 1\rangle$ is noted A') and elements of V_N° are noted as uppercase roman letters without a prime (e.g. $\langle A, 0\rangle$ is noted A).

Figure 4.1 below provides an example of a derivation in an MCFG. For MCFGs, we can consider derivations as such to be the relevant structural descriptions.

---

[1] The idea of marking items in phrase structure based theories in order to obtain dependency type interpretations can be traced to three sources (at least): the use of the superscript w by Gaifman (1965:319-320) to mark head daughters in CFGs, X-bar grammar (Chomsky 1970), and the marked constituent systems of Gladkii 1970.

[2] See above 2.5.2. This restriction is for simplicity in stating the relevant results. Obviously, it is possible to allow syncategorematic terminals, and to have special clauses in the relevant Interpretation Functions to ensure that they get interpreted in an appropriate way with respect to dependency and constituency.

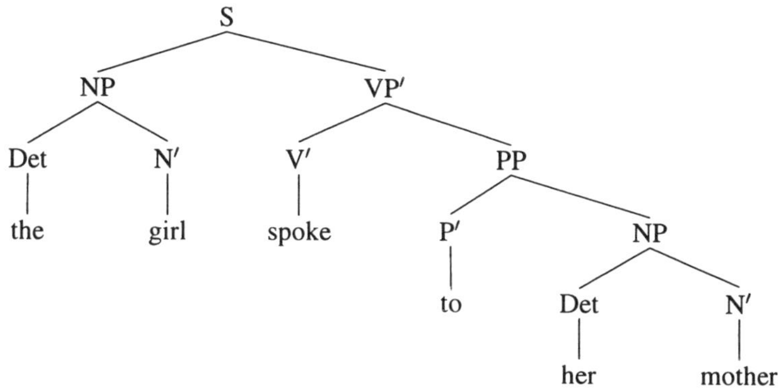

Figure 4.1

MCFGs have legitimate interpretations in terms of constituency and dependency. For constituency, this is obvious, and the Interpretation Function $IF_{CFG \to C}$ used for ordinary CFGs will do the job. For dependency, we can define as in (2) the Interpretation Function $IF_{MCFG \to D}$ which maps a structural description in an MCFG to the intended dependency relation.

(2) $IF_{MCFG \to D} : \Sigma(MCFG) \to ID_D : \sigma \to R$ where an occurrence o depends on the occurrence o', $o' \neq o$, such that there is a node n such that (i) $n \in V_N^{\circ}$; (ii) n dominates both o and o'; (iii) the nodes on the path from n to o' all belong to V_N'; and (iv) n is the lowest node in the tree with properties (i), (ii) and (iii).

This choice of Interpretation Function assigns the following dependency relation to the sentence generated in Figure 4.1 above.

(3) 

Given the constraint on the distribution of marked nonterminals in the productions of MCFGs and the choice of the Interpretation Function in (2), it is obvious that MCFGs can express exactly the same range of dependency relations on strings as DGs in the sense of section 3.6.1.4 (cf. (2.17), (2.18) of chapter 2). Specifically, we have (4), and consequently (5).

(4) MCFGs can express all and only the dependency relations R on a string of occurrences ζ such that R is an irreflexive, asymetric,

intransitive relation on ζ, and such that (a) there is one occurrence in ζ which does not depend on any other occurrence; (b) every other occurrence in ζ depends on one and only one other occurrence; and (c) for any occurrence in ζ, that occurrence and all the occurrences which depend on it directly or indirectly form a continuous substring of ζ.

(5) $IF_{MCFG \to D}(\Sigma(MCFG)) = IF_{DG \to D}(\Sigma(DG))$

The occurrence specified in (4a) is the *head* or *independent* occurrence of the string.

Theorem (6) characterizes the possible pairings of dependency and constituency that can be assigned to strings of occurrences by derivations in MCFGs.

(6) Given a string of occurrences ζ, an MCFG G can assign to ζ a dependency relation R satisfying conditions (4) and a constituency structure Γ satisfying conditions (2.4a, b, c) and (2.9) of Chapter 2 if and only if, in every constituent defined by Γ, R is such that there is one and only one occurrence which does not depend on an occurrence inside that constituent and all the other occurrences in the constituent depend directly or indirectly on that occurrence.

PROOF

I. It is obvious that any tree in Σ(MCFG) satisfies the condition in (6), given the way $IF_{MCFG \to D}$ is defined in (2), and the constraints on the form of productions in (1).

II. For the opposite direction, we need to show that for any pair $\langle\Gamma, R\rangle$ satisfying (6), there is an MCFG that generates a structural description expressing $\langle\Gamma, R\rangle$. Given Γ, we can construct a tree which defines Γ as a constituent structure on the string (indeed Γ satisfies the relevant conditions for this namely (2.4, 2.9) of chapter 2). We show by construction that the tree can be marked so as to define R. Starting from the root, do the following inductively on all nodes n of the tree, by order of increasing depth of embedding: By hypothesis, the constituent dominated by n contains one and only one occurrence which which does not depend on an occurrence inside that constituent; mark the daughter of n which dominates that occurrence. This obviously gives us a tree in Σ(MCFG), which expresses R on its terminal string. ■

The following theorems can be proved on the relationships between MCFGs, DGs and CFGs:

(7) MCFGs are equivalent to CFGs and DGs in WGC.

(8) MCFGs are equivalent in SGC to CFGs with respect to constituency interpretations.[3]

(9) The theory of DGs is strictly included in SGC in the theory of MCFGs with respect to constituency interpretations.

(10) The theory of DGs is strictly included in SGC in the theory of MCFGs with respect to dependency interpretations. Specifically, an MCFG G has an equivalent DG G' if and only if G is of finite degree.

(11) The theory of DGs is strictly included in SGC in the theory of MCFGs with respect to the pair of constituency and dependency interpretations.

Theorem (7) is obvious, given the weak equivalence of CFGs and DGs, as is (8). (9) follows immediately from theorem (2.22) of section 2.12. The notion of *degree* in theorem (10) is from Gaifman 1965. Theorem (10) is a direct consequence of theorems (17) and (21) of section 4.1.3 below. We put off further discussion of this theorem to that section. As for (11), it is a direct consequence of (9) and(10).

Note that it would be possible to define a variant of MCFGs allowing more than one marked element on the right hand side of productions, interpreting the resulting structures as multiheaded (this would allow a formalization of the analysis of coordination as a multiheaded construction proposed e.g. in Sag et al. 1985). This would lead to more complex dependency relations than we have explored here, since one occurrence would be allowed to depend on more than one other occurrence, e.g. the object would be interpreted as depending on both verbs in a structure with a coordination of verbs, such as *John cooked and ate steaks.*

4.1.2 Weakly Marked CFGs (WMCFGs)

WMCFGs are similar to MCFGs, except that productions P are such that at most one element on the right hand side belongs to V_N' (i.e.

---

[3] MCFGs are incommensurable in SGC to CFGs with respect to labeled constituency if the Interpretation Function for labeled constituency is set up so as to assign pairs $\langle A, n\rangle$ as labels. An alternative would be to consider marking as irrelevant to constituent labeling, and to define the Interpretation Function so that it simply assigns the first element of the pair as the label. In this case, MCFGs are obviously strongly equivalent to CFGs with respect to labeled constituency.

is marked), rather than one and only one; that is productions of type (12) are allowed on top of those allowed in (1a, b).

(12) $\forall p \in P, p = A \rightarrow B_1 \dots B_n, A \in V_N, B_1 \dots B_n \in V_N' \cup V_N^\circ$ and $\neg\exists i, j, i \neq j \mid B_i, B_j \in V_N'$.

Using the Interpretation Function $IF_{MCFG \rightarrow D}$ given in (2), WMCFGs define dependency relations on strings which can violate condition (6). Namely it can happen that there is more than one occurrence in a constituent which does not depend on an occurrence inside that constituent. For this to be the case, it is necessary and sufficient that there be no marked daughters in the local tree whose terminal string is that constituent. In the case where the local tree comprising the root has no marked daughter, this will lead to there being more than one independent occurrence (unless the root has only one daughter). Such a dependency relation will be called *partial*. Obviously, apart from the single independent occurrence constraint, constraints on dependency relations R expressed by WMCFGs are the same as for dependency relations defined by DGs (viz. R is irreflexive, asymetric, intransitive; any occurrence depends on at most one occurrence; for every occurrence, that occurrence and all those occurrences which depend on it directly or indirectly form a continuous substring). For instance, $IF_{MCFG \rightarrow D}$ applied to the structural description in Figure 4.2, results in the partial dependency relation in (13).

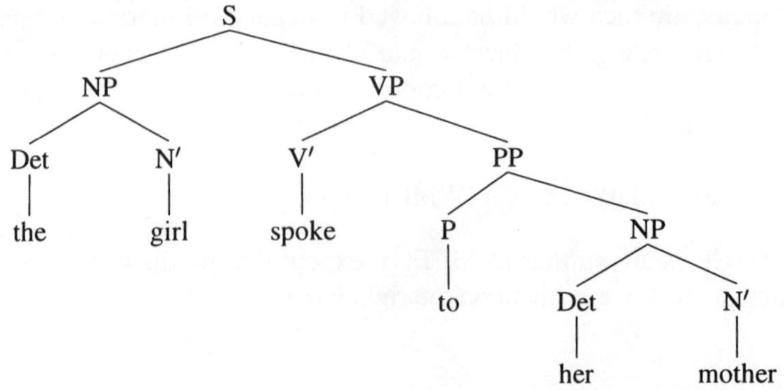

Figure 4.2

(13) The girl spoke to her mother

Because neither the NP nor the VP daughter of S is marked, and there is no node dominating both NP and VP which also directly dominates a node labeled with an element of $V_N{}'$, $\mathrm{IF}_{\mathrm{MCFG}\rightarrow\mathrm{D}}$ results in neither of the two occurrences *girl* or *spoke* depending on the other, nor on any third occurrence; both are independent occurrences. Similarly, because neither the P nor the NP daughter of PP is marked, neither *to* depends on *mother* nor *mother* on *to*. Both depend on *spoke*, which is outside the PP constituent.

We can prove the following theorems about the dependency relations definable by WMCFGs:

(14) DGs and MCFGs are strictly included in SGC in WMCFGs with respect to dependency interpretations.

(15) MCFGs are strictly included in SGC in WMCFGs with respect to the pair of dependency and constituency interpretations.

The first is obvious, given (10) and the fact that the MCFGs are strictly included in the WMCFGs, since beyond the dependency structures with only a single independent occurrence, to which DGs and MCFGs are restricted, WMCFGs also allow dependency structures with more than one independent occurrence. The second is equally obvious, since WMCFGs can generate pairings of dependency and constituency structures which do not satisfy condition (6).

4.1.3 Strongly Marked CFGs (SMCFGs)

SMCFGs are a variant of MCFGs obtained by adding a special constraint on well formed derivations.[4] Namely, marked nonterminals can only be rewritten by productions of the type $B \rightarrow b$ where $b \in V_T$.[5]

(16) $\phi\, B'\, \psi \Rightarrow \phi\, \xi\, \psi$, where $B' \in V_N{}'$ and $\phi, \xi, \psi \in (V_N{}' \cup V_N{}^{\circ} \cup V_T)^*$ if and only if there is a production $B \rightarrow \xi$ in P and $\xi \in V_T$

4 The idea of SMCFG has its source in the strongly marked constituent systems discussed in Dominicy 1982, as a variant of Gladkii 1970's marked constituent systems.

5 The reason why this condition cannot be stated as a condition on productions is that productions have been defined so that their left hand side does not take account of marking (cf. (1)).

Marked nonterminals are consequently necessarily preterminals. The Interpretation Function for dependency for SMCFGs is the same as for MCFGs (i.e. $IF_{MCFG \rightarrow D}$ given in (2)). We can illustrate SMCFGs with the derivation given in Figure 4.3 below, which assigns the same dependency structure (3) to its terminal string as Figure 4.1, but assigns a different, 'flatter', constituent structure.

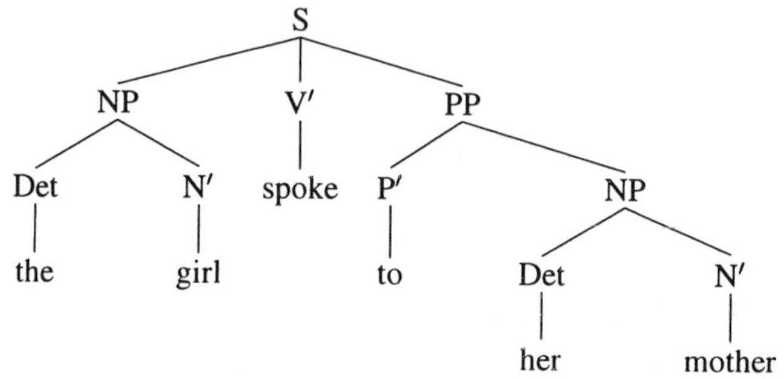

Figure 4.3

Theorem (17) establishes the strong equivalence of SMCFGs and DGs.

(17) SMCFGs are equivalent in SGC to DGs with respect to pairs of constituency and dependency interpretations.

Before proving this theorem, let us first note that MCFGs can also be defined so that node labels are understood as atomic symbols from two distinct nonterminal vocabularies, $V_N{}^{\circ}$ and $V_N{}'$, respectively the unmarked and marked nonterminal vocabularies. We define V_N as $V_N{}' \cup V_N{}^{\circ}$ Under these hypotheses, an MCFG is a 5-tuple $G = \langle V_N{}', V_N{}^{\circ}, V_T, S, P \rangle$, where $S \in V_N{}^{\circ}$ (i.e., the initial symbol is non-marked), similar to a CFG but with the following further constraint on productions in P, beyond those usual for CFGs.

(18) $\forall p \in P$, either

a. $p = A \rightarrow B_1 \ldots B_n \mid A \in V_N{}' \cup V_N{}^{\circ}, \exists! i, 1 \leq i \leq n \mid B_i \in V_N{}'$ and $\forall B_j\ 1 \leq j \leq n$ and $j \neq i, B_j \in V_N{}^{\circ}$; or

b. $p = A \rightarrow a \mid A \in V_N{}' \cup V_N{}^{\circ}$ and $a \in V_T$.

Under this definition of MCFG, the special restriction defining SMCFGs can be expressed as a constraint on the form of productions, rather than on derivations, namely:

(19) $\forall B' \in V_N', \forall p \in P$, if $p = B' \rightarrow x$, then $x \in V_T$

This is possible because under these definitions, contrary to those chosen above, productions apply specifically either to members of V_N° or of V_N'.

These alternative definitions are obviously equivalent to the original ones for constituency and dependency interpretations.[6] I will use them in the rest of this section because they allow a simpler statement of the proofs to be given.

Given the alternative definition of SMCFGs, it is very easy to prove theorem (17) by construction. We first show that for every SMCFG G, there is a strongly equivalent DG G' with respect to constituency and dependency.

PROOF

Let $G = \langle V_N', V_N^{\circ}, V_T, S, P\rangle$. We define $G' = \langle V_N, V_T, D, L, T\rangle$ as follows: V_N of $G' = V_N' \cup V_N^{\circ}$ of G. For all rules of type $A \rightarrow a$ in P of G, $A \in V_N$, add the lexical rule $A \rightarrow a$ in L of G'. For all rules of type $A \rightarrow B_1 \ldots B_n$ where B_i is the unique member of V_N' on the right hand side, add the rule $A\ (B_1, \ldots, B_{i\text{-}1} * B_{i+1}, \ldots, B_n)$ in D of G'.

It is obvious that these two grammars generate the same set of sentences assigning them the same pairs of interpretations in terms of constituency and dependency, using the Interpretation Function for constituency given in (2.21) of chapter 2 for DGs. ■

Given this construction, the opposite construction is obvious, and it is clear that there is also a strongly equivalent SMCFG for every DG, with respect to pairs of constituency and dependency interpretations. Theorem (17) is consequently proved. Note furthermore that (20) is a consequence of (7), of (17) and of the weak equivalence of CFGs and DGs.

(20) CFGs, MCFGs, WMCFGs, SMCFGs and DGs are equivalent in WGC.

Theorem (21) establishes the inclusion of SMCFGs in MCFGs with respect to both constituency and dependency interpretations.

(21) SMCFGs are strictly included in SGC in MCFGs with respect to both constituency and dependency interpretations.

---

[6] Note however that they lead to problems in the definition of endocentricity interpretations, discussed in section 4.3 below. This is the main reason for preferring the original definition.

Strict inclusion with respect to constituency is obvious, given the constraint (19) on productions in SMCFGs (or, equivalently, constraint (16) on well formed derivations under the initial definition). Strict inclusion with respect to dependency is a more interesting and complicated result to obtain. Let us first note that at the level of the formalisms, SMCFGs express the same range of interpretations with respect to dependency as do MCFGs, in the sense of section 3.6.1.4.

(22) $IF_{MCFG \rightarrow D}(\Sigma(MCFG)) = IF_{MCFG \rightarrow D}(\Sigma(SMCFG))$

This is a direct consequence of theorems (5) and (17). However, the second part of (21) is true because there are MCFGs which can generate sets of strings, assigning them dependency interpretations such that no SMCFG generates the same sets with the same dependency interpretations. More specifically, we prove the following theorems:

(23) An MCFG G has a strongly equivalent SMCFG G', with respect to dependency, if and only if there is a finite upper bound on the length of head-paths in $\Sigma(G)$.

(24) An MCFG G has a strongly equivalent SMCFG* G', with respect to dependency, if all unbounded head paths in $\Sigma(G)$ involve either only right-headed or only left-headed productions.[7]

Let us first define the new concepts appearing in these theorems. A *head-path* in a derivation in an MCFG is a path of nodes $\langle N_1, ..., N_k \rangle$, $k \geq 1$, such that (a) N_i directly dominates N_{i+1}, $1 \leq i < k$; (b) all the nodes $N_1, ..., N_k$ are marked; (c) N_1 is not directly dominated by a marked node; (d) N_k is a preterminal node. For example, in Figure 4.1 above, ⟨VP′, V′⟩, ⟨P′⟩ and ⟨N′⟩ are head paths. Obviously, the minimal MCFG with the set of productions necessary to generate Figure 4.1 has a finite bound on the length of head paths. On the other hand, the MCFG G with productions $S \rightarrow S'S$, and $S \rightarrow a$ does not have a finite bound on the length of head paths, as evidenced in Figure 4.4. There is no upper limit on paths of marked nodes S'.

[7] Note that the satisfaction of this condition is decidable.

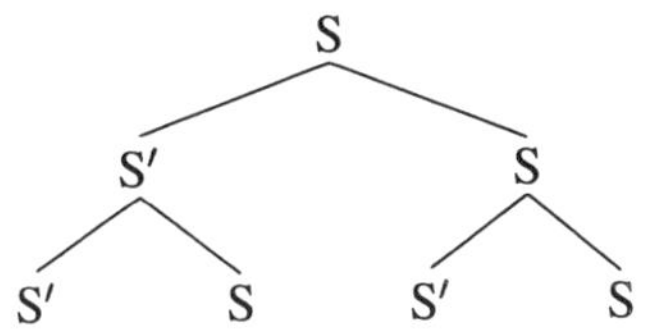

Figure 4.4

We define a *right-headed* (respectively *left-headed*) production in an MCFG as a production where the rightmost (respectively leftmost) element on the right-hand side is the marked element. Finally, let us define an SMCFG* as an SMCFG where the right-hand side may be defined using regular expressions over the nonterminal vocabularies. The idea of allowing infinite rule schemata of this type goes back to Chomsky and Miller (1963: 298), who propose such a schema for coordination. Langendoen 1976 shows that we do not increase the WGC beyond that of simple CFGs by allowing infinite grammars with such regular expressions schematically defining the right-hand sides of CF productions.

Before proving (23) and (24), let me introduce one further useful concept. Let us define a *spine* as a tree where, at each level of embedding, a single sister is rewritten, and such that the most deeply embedded local tree has a daughter which is a preterminal (i.e. a daughter A, $A \in V_N$, such that there is a rule of type, $A \rightarrow a$, where $a \in V_T$. The *yield* of a spine S, $y(S)$, is consequently of the form $\phi A \psi$, where $\phi, \psi \in V_N^*$ and A is a preterminal. Figure 4.5 is an example of a spine, the yield of which is *NP V′ PP*.

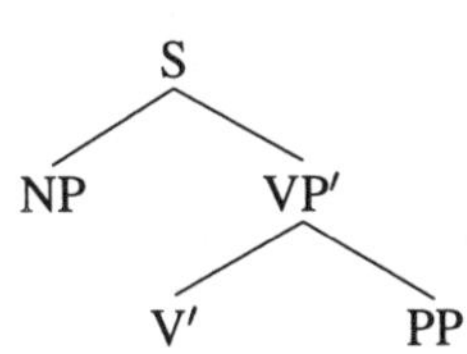

Figure 4.5

Let us now prove theorem (23).[8] We first prove, in I, that if an MCFG G_1 is such that there is a finite bound on the length of head paths in $\Sigma(G_1)$, there is a strongly equivalent SMCFG G_2 with respect to dependency. The intuition is that the finite bound on head paths makes it possible to create a grammar G_2 that collapses head paths so that they are reduced to a single node, which has as its sisters all of the sisters of the nodes on the head path of the original grammar. Then, in II, we show that this is a necessary condition.

PROOF

I. Consider the subset T of elements of V_N° of G_1 such that there are productions of type (18a) (i.e. $A \rightarrow B_1 \ldots B_n$) which have these elements as their left-hand sides. The elements in T can immediately dominate the top of a head path. Given that the set of productions P of G_1 is finite, and that there is a finite bound on the length of head paths in $\Sigma(G)$, it is clear that, for each element t of T, G_1 defines a finite set HP(t) of head paths that can be directly dominated by t, and that furthermore that set of head paths defines a finite set SP(t) of spines rooted in t, and such that the path from root to terminal in the spines is in HP(t). Finally, each t in T defines a finite set of strings $Y = y(\mathrm{SP}(t))$ which are the yields of the spines in SP(t). Note that the strings in Y necessarily satisfy the conditions on right-hand sides of productions in MCFGs, namely there is one and only one element belonging to V_N'.

We define the production set of G_2 as follows: it contains all of the productions in P of G_1 which have an unmarked element on their left hand side, as well as all the productions of type $A \rightarrow a$, $a \in V_T$. Furthermore it contains all of the productions $t \rightarrow x$, where $t \in T$ and $x \in y(\mathrm{SP}(t))$. It is clear that G_2 will generate the same set of strings as G_1, assigning them the same dependency relations. Indeed, what we have done is essentially to create a grammar that collapses head paths so that they are reduced to a single node, which has as sisters all the sisters of the nodes on the head path of the original grammar. ■

Figure 4.6a illustrates how a set of productions leading to a bounded head path is replaced by a single production (25), which gives rise to the corresponding tree in Figure 4.6b, with the collapsed head path $\langle A', F' \rangle$. Note also that Figure 4.3 above results from Figure 4.1 by just such a collapsing of the ⟨VP′, V′⟩ head path.

---

[8] Gaifman 1965 proves a closely related theorem (his (3.10)). However, because of the way he defines the problem, his proof is more complex, and less perspicuous.

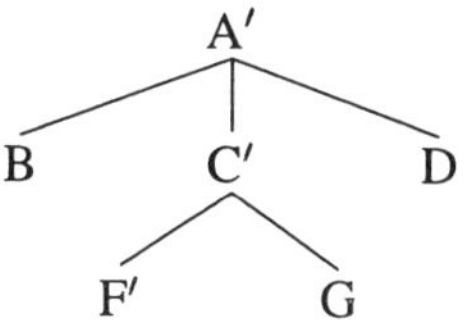

Figure 4.6a

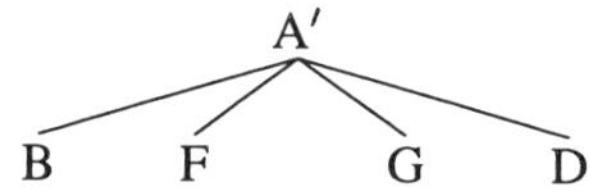

Figure 4.6b

(25) A → B F′ G D

PROOF

II. Consider a grammar G_1 which allows unbounded head paths in $\Sigma(G_1)$. If t is an element of $V_N{}^\circ$ which can directly dominate such unbounded head paths, then t can obviously be the root of a set of spines SP(t), in which the path from root to preterminal contains only marked elements, and such that the length of this path is unbounded in the set. Consequently, there is no bound on the length of the strings in y(SP(t)).[9] But, given the way dependency is defined in MCFGs, for each spine in SP(t), each nonterminal in y(SP(t)), except the designated preterminal at the foot of the spine, must dominate (directly or indirectly) a terminal which directly depends on the daughter of the designated preterminal. Consequently, if there are unbounded head paths in $\Sigma(G_1)$ there is no bound in $\Sigma(G_1)$ on the number of occurrences which can depend on a given occurrence. But obviously, in SMCFGs with a finite number of productions, there always is such a bound. Specifically, if $p = A \rightarrow x$ is the production with the longest right-hand side in an SMCFG, then $|x| - 1$ is the maximum number of occurrences which can directly depend on a given occurrence. It is thus clear that the existence of a finite bound on head paths in the derivation set of an MCFG is necessary for there to be a strongly equivalent SMCFG with respect to dependency. ■

Let us now turn to theorem (24). As is made clear in the preceding proof, the crucial problem for SMCFGs is that they cannot characterize

[9] Note that for this to be true, we have to eliminate non-branching productions leading to subderivations of the type $A \Rightarrow^* A$. This can be done in full generality, without affecting the labeled constituency or dependency interpretations of the grammar.

systems where the number of possible dependents on a given occurrence is unbounded. The use of infinite rule schemata is an obvious strategy to try to overcome this limitation. We consider the extension of SMCFG where the right hand side of productions is allowed to be a regular expression on $V_N' \cup V_N^{\circ} \cup V_T$, which we call SMCFG*. We prove by construction that an MCFG G_1 has a strongly equivalent SMCFG* G_2, with respect to dependency, if all unbounded head paths in $\Sigma(G)$ involve either only right-headed or only left-headed productions. The preceding theorem shows how to deal with bounded head paths. We will limit our attention here to the case of unbounded head paths.

PROOF

Consider the subset T of elements of V_N° of G_1 which can directly dominate a set of unbounded head paths. By hypothesis, we know that for every t in T, HP(t), the set of unbounded head paths that can be directly dominated by t, can be divided into two subsets, LHP(t) and RHP(t), which respectively contain head paths involving only left-headed and only right-headed productions. Let us define LP(t) (resp. RP(t)) as the set of productions which can be used in producing the spines LSP(t) (resp. RSP(t)) associated with LHP(t) (resp. RHP(t)). It is possible, for every t in T, to define a finite sets of productions LP′(t) and RP′(t) on the basis of LP(t) and RP(t), such that LP′(t) (resp. RP′(t)) defines a set of spines LSP′(t) (resp. RSP′(t)) and y(LSP(t)) = y(LSP′(t)) (resp y(RSP(t)) = y(RSP′(t))), and such that no two productions in LP′(t) (resp RP′(t)) have the same marked element on the right hand side. As a result of this construction, for every t in T, LP′(t) (resp. RP′(t)) generates a set of spines which is the tree set of a CFG LG′(t) (resp. RG′(t)), having LP′(t) (resp. RP′(t)) as its rule set, and where the unmarked nonterminals are interpreted as terminals. It is known that the path set of the tree set of a CFG is a regular language (cf. Thatcher 1973). Consequently, the set of head paths that can be directly dominated by t is the union of two regular languages, and can be characterized by the regular expressions LR(t) and RR(t). Now, given that for both of these, the productions involved are either all right-headed or all left-headed, it is trivial to define a regular expression LR′(t) (resp. RR′(t)) which characterizes the yield of the set of spines y(LSP′(t)) (resp. y(RSP′(t))). We can now define the production set of G_2, so that it contains all the productions of G_1 which have an unmarked element on their left hand side, as well as all the productions of type $A \rightarrow a$. Furthermore, we add all the productions of the type $t \rightarrow$ LR′(t) and $t \rightarrow$ RR′(t). Obviously, the grammar thus constructed is strongly equivalent to the original grammar with respect to dependency, as desired. ■

Let us illustrate this construction for the MCFG G_1, $V_N' = \{S'\}$, $V_N^\circ = \{S\}$, $V_T = \{a\}$, $P = \{S \to S'S, S' \to S'S, S \to a, S' \to a\}$. This grammar generates derivations with unbounded head paths, as illustrated in boldface in Figure 4.7.

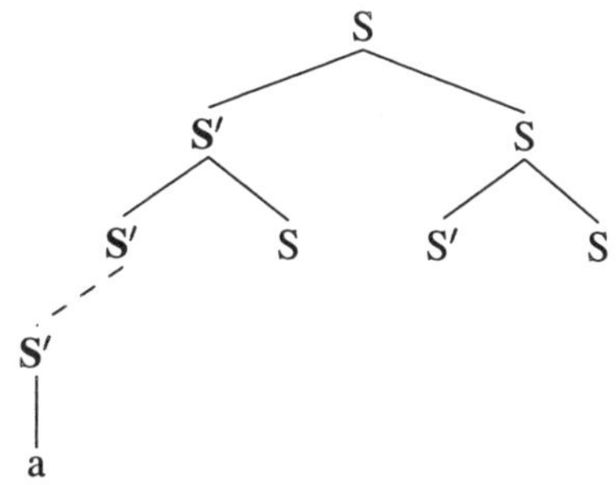

Figure 4.7

For G_1, we have $T = \{S\}$, LP(S) = LP′(S) = $\{S' \to S'S\}$, LR(S) = S'^*, LR′(S) = y(SP(S)) = $S'S^*$. Consequently, our construction yields the SMCFG G_2 with $V_N' = \{S'\}$, $V_N^\circ = \{S\}$, $V_T = \{a\}$, $P = \{S \to S'S^*$, $S \to a, S' \to a\}$. Figure 4.8a and 4.8b show corresponding derivations in G_1 and G_2 respectively for the generation of the string *aaaa*, where the dependency relation assigned has the three last occurrences directly depending on the first.

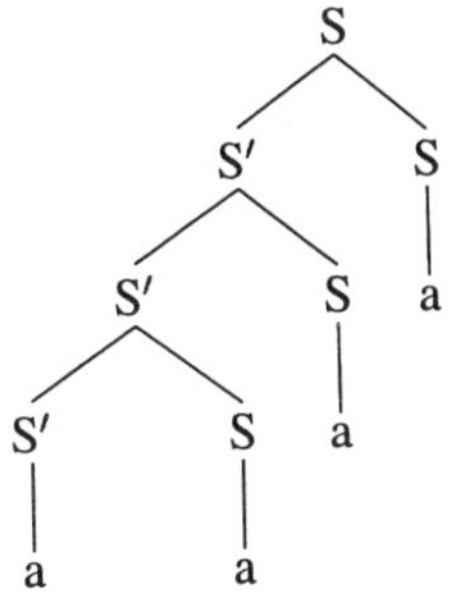

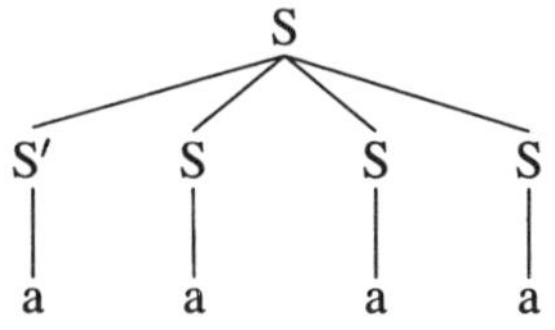

Figure 4.8a

Figure 4.8b

The main insight of the preceding discussion is that it is not possible to assign an unbounded number of dependents to a given occurrence with phrase structure grammars using finite productions and with bounds on the lengths of head paths. This insight will be important in our discussion of X-bar grammars in the following section. To conclude this discussion, let us return to theorem (10) of section 4.1.1, which establishes the strong inclusion of DGs in MCFGs with respect to dependency. This theorem follows directly from the preceding theorem (21), given the strong equivalence of DGs and SMCFGs established in (17). Furthermore, it should be noted that we can characterize the MCFGs for which there is an equivalent DG with respect to dependency by theorems parallel to (23) and (24), provided we define a variant of DG, DG*, allowing infinite dependency rule schemata where the dependents are given by regular expressions over nonterminals.

4.1.4 X-bar Grammars

Kornai and Pullum 1990 define six basic properties characteristic of X-bar grammars (XBGs, originally proposed in Chomsky 1970), which I state here informally for reference in subsequent discussion (for technical details, and extended bibliographical references see the original article).

- **Lexicality**. Every nonterminal is of the form X^i, where X^0 is a lexical category, and $i \geq 0$.
- **Succession**. All rules rewriting some nonterminal X^n have a daughter labeled X^{n-1}.
- **Uniformity**. The maximal bar level is the same for every preterminal (we use m to designate that bar level in uniformity observing grammars).
- **Maximality**. All non-head daughters are maximal projections.
- **Centrality**. The start symbol is the maximal projection of a distinguished preterminal.
- **Optionality**. All non-head daughters are optional.

Kornai and Pullum identify the notion of head (and consequently of dependency) as the central content of X-bar theory. The tree in Figure 4.9 is understood to define the dependency relation given in (26) on its terminal string.[10]

[10] I am using dependency between occurrences here as elsewhere in this study, rather than c-dependency, which is the more usual way of thinking of dependency in the XBG tradition. Recall though that the two notions are interdefinable (cf. section 2.8 above).

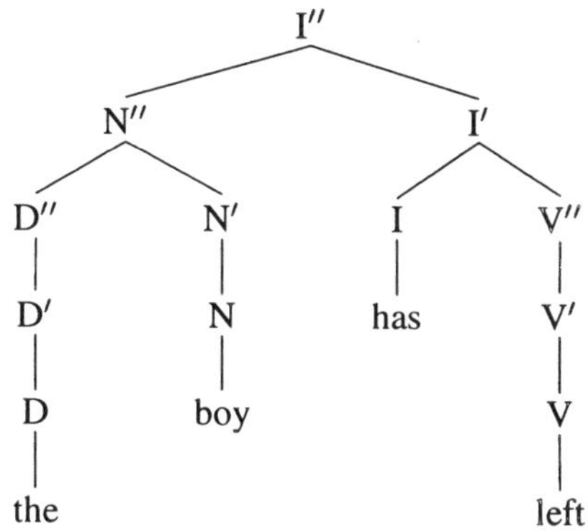

Figure 4.9

(26) The boy has left

The Interpretation Function given in (27) assigns dependency interpretations[11] to X-bar structural descriptions in keeping with the classical understanding of the notion *head* in XBG.[12]

(27) $IF_{XBG \rightarrow D} : \Sigma(XBG) \rightarrow ID_D : \sigma \rightarrow R$ such that the occurrence which has the root node as its maximal projection is the head of the string and all other occurrences *o* depend on the occurrence *o′* such that the maximal projection of *o* is both the sister and the daughter of a projection of *o′*.

Kornai and Pullum claim that 'maintaining the SXBG conditions [Standard X-Bar Grammar conditions, i.e. Lexicality, Maximality and Succession, PHM] commits a linguist to nothing at all as regards limits

---

[11] Note that if you allow multiheaded structures (e.g. in coordination), you will get dependency relations of the type discussed at the end of section 4.1.1. In this case, the Interpretation Function (27) must be modified.

[12] It should be noted that the definition of XBG given by Kornai and Pullum (1990: 26), does not in fact support a legitimate dependency interpretation as defined in section 2.15 above. This is because it does not explicitly provide for distinctions corresponding to bar level within the nonterminal vocabulary, and consequently bar level information will be lost under arbitrary relabeling. Note though that any definition which incorporates such distinctions into the definition will work, e.g. those of Bresnan 1976, or GKPS.

on what is describable by CFGs' (Kornai and Pullum 1990: 42). In what follows, I will show that the conception of SGC defended here allows us to prove that, in fact, XBGs have a quite different expressive power from CFGs, both with respect to constituency, and with respect to dependency. I will show this for X-bar Grammars respecting Lexicality, Maximality, Succession and Uniformity. Though the latter is not crucial to the demonstration, it makes it simpler;[13] henceforth, unless otherwise stated, I use XBG to refer to the set of grammars respecting those four conditions.

To start with, as was noted in section 2.14, CFGs as classically defined do not allow a relevant legitimate dependency interpretation. One can try to circumvent this difficulty by proposing a comparison between XBGs and MCFGs, rather than simple CFGs, and interpreting the head node in any local tree in an X-bar structural description in the same way as a marked element in an MCFG. But, even with such a revision, Kornai and Pullum's claim does not hold. The crucial factor that underlies the difference in expressive power between XBGs and CFGs is the fact that the path of nonterminals from any preterminal node to its Maximal Projection will comprise $m + 1$ nodes. This is a direct consequence of Succession (we will discuss the consequences of adopting a Weaker version of Succession below). There is no corresponding constraint on MCFGs, restricting the length of paths of marked elements (called *head-paths* in the preceding section).

Note however, that the class of XBGs with maximal projection level $m = 1$ (henceforth XBG^1) is strongly equivalent to SMCFGs with respect to the pair of constituency and dependency interpretations. Intuitively, the bar notation is simply the reverse of the mark notation. It is easy to show that for any XBG^1 there is an SMCFG strongly equivalent with respect to constituency and dependency. To construct the equivalent SMCFG, simply consider all bar-0 items in productions as marked, and all bar-1 items as unmarked. The new grammar will generate the same tree set as the original XBG^1, and obviously assign the same dependency relations. Showing that for any SMCFG G there is an XBG^1 G' which is strongly equivalent with respect to constituency and dependency is also easy. One must simply take adequate precautions so that the resulting grammar conforms to the XBG constraints on labeling. The following construction will do the job.

---

[13] To get the results below for grammars not respecting Uniformity, simply consider m in the discussion to be the highest of the various maximal bar-levels, rather than the unique maximal bar-level.

For every production $A \rightarrow \psi\, B'\, \phi$ in P of G, where $\psi, \phi \in V_N{}^{\circ *}$, and $B' \in V_N'$, create a rule $B^1 \rightarrow \psi^1\, B^0\, \phi^1$, in a rule set P°, where ψ^1, ϕ^1 are the strings of categories ψ, ϕ with bar level 1, and add B^1 to the set of replacements for A. From the set of productions P° thus obtained, construct the rule set P' of G' by replacing, under all possible combinations, the elements in ϕ, ψ in the different rules of P° by the elements in their sets of replacements. Furthermore, for any unmarked category $A \in V_N{}^\circ$ in G, for which there are productions of the type $A \rightarrow a$ in P, add the corresponding productions $A^0 \rightarrow a$ to P' and, if $A \in V_N'$, the production $A^1 \rightarrow A^0$. For any marked category $A' \in V_N'$ in G, for which there are productions of type $A' \rightarrow a$, add the production $A^0 \rightarrow a$ to P'. It is obvious that the resulting grammar G' generates the same set of strings as G, assigning them the same constituent structures and dependency relations.

We can illustrate the above construction of an XBG^1 from an SMCFG by applying it to the grammar implicit in the generation of Figure 4.3 above. This gives us the result in Figure 4.10.

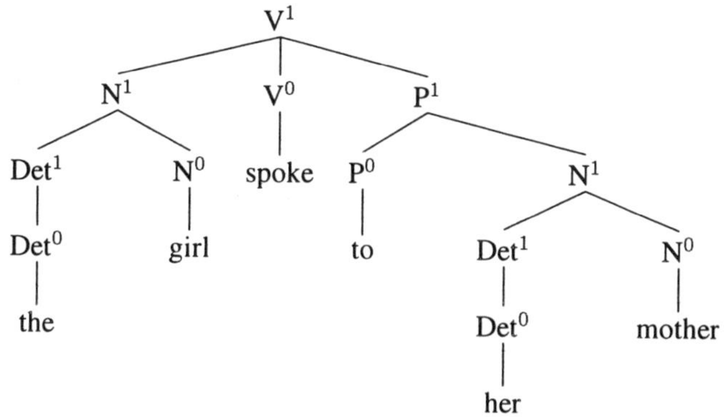

Figure 4.10

Note that labeling properties of the MCFG are crucially not preserved by this construction. We thus have the theorems in (28).

(28) a. The class of SMCFG is strongly equivalent to the class of X-bar Grammars with maximal projection level 1 (XGB^1) with respect to pairs of dependency and constituency interpretations.

b. The class of DGs is strongly equivalent to the class of X-bar Grammars with maximal projection level 1 (XGB^1) with respect to pairs of dependency and constituency interpretations.

c. The class of XBGs satisfying Lexicality, Maximality, Succession and Uniformity are strictly included in SGC in MCFGs both with respect to dependency and with respect to constituency interpretations.

We can obtain an infinite hierarchy of XBGs based on the choice of m, with XBG^1 equivalent with respect to dependency and constituency to SMCFG, and where $\Sigma(XBG^m)$ is strongly included in Σ(MCFG) for all maximal bar levels m, with respect to dependency and constituency. This is illustrated in Figure 4.11.

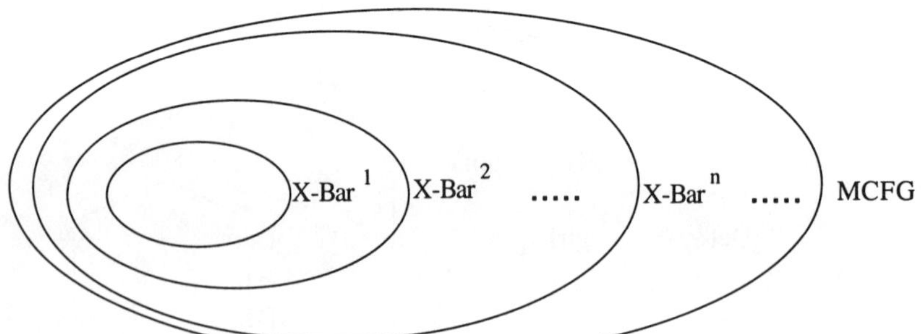

Figure 4.11. The hierarchy of SXBGs

For all XBGs, irrespective of choice of m, there is an MCFG which is equivalent with respect to constituency and dependency, which can be constructed in a parallel way to the construction given above for XBG^1. However, there are MCFGs which are beyond the reach of any XBG with finite m. This will be the case for all MCFGs that allow unbounded paths of marked elements (i.e. head-paths) in their derivation sets (for instance, presence of a rule $A' \rightarrow A' B$ is sufficient to allow such unbounded paths). Consequently, it is obvious that XBGs are strictly included in MCFGs for SGC both with respect to constituency and with respect to dependency, as stated in (28c).

It should be noted here that allowing Weak Succession[14] (rather than Succession), i.e. allowing for productions $X^k \to \psi\ X^j\ \phi$, $k \geq j$ (rather than $k > j$), is not sufficient to make XBG equivalent to MCFG. Allowing Weak Succession removes the restriction on derivations in XBGs to the effect that the path from a terminal to its maximal projection is bounded. However, even with this restriction lifted, the constraints on labeling imposed by XBGs make them less expressive with respect to constituency than MCFGs, because XBG forces all the nodes on the head path to be projections of the *same* lexical category. This can be demonstrated as follows. Consider the following rules in an MCFG, generating structures like Figure 4.12.

(29) $A' \to D\ B'$ $\qquad B' \to A'\ E$

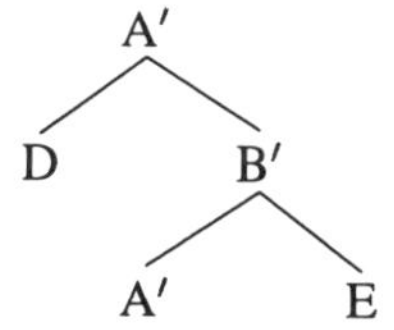

Figure 4.12

Figure 4.12 can be unboundedly embedded in itself, leading to unboundedly long paths of marked nonterminals. If the grammar contains no further rules rewriting A' and B', these paths will always be such that nonmarked sister nodes will appear alternately on the left and right of the path of marked items (specifically, to the right if the marked item is A' and to the left if it is B'), as shown in Figure 4.13 overleaf.

Any XBG, with Weak Succession, attempting to simulate such an MCFG will have to allow for unbounded embeddings of adjunction structures (i.e. structures where a mother has the same bar level as its head daughter). Furthermore, since the path of marked categories is unbounded in the MCFG, there will be have to be unbounded embeddings of adjunctions at at least one bar-level, and that, whatever the choice of the maximal bar level m. For concreteness let us assume that $m = 2$, and that there is an unbounded embedding of adjunctions at the level of A^1.

---

[14] Cf. Kornai and Pullum (1990: 29). Linguistically, Weak Succession is necessary if one wants to allow adjunction structures of the form $[_A\ x\ [_A\ y]]$.

Under these conditions the corresponding XBG will generate structures like that in Figure 4.14, corresponding to Figure 4.13.

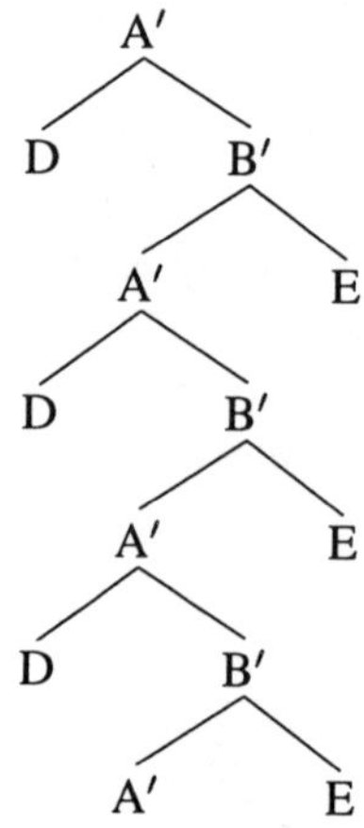

Figure 4.13

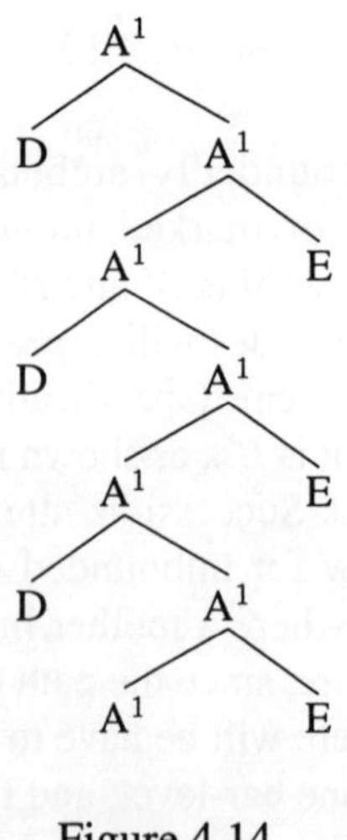

Figure 4.14

This means that the XBG will have the productions (30).

(30) $A' \rightarrow D\ A'$ $A' \rightarrow A'\ E$

But there is nothing in such a grammar fragment that can enforce the appearance of nonhead sisters on alternate sides of the head path, as was the case in the original MCFG. An XBG with rules (30) will be able to generate structures where this constraint is violated. Thus, an XBG, even with Weak Succession, is incapable of generating the same range of constituent structures as MCFGs (note that this is true of simple, non-labeled constituent structures: though it is the labeling constraints on XBG that result in this weaker expressive power, the weakness is present at the level of simple constituency). We thus obtain the following theorem.

(31) XBGs with weak succession are strictly included in SGC in MCFGs with respect to constituency interpretations.

Kornai and Pullum (1990:42) note that 'Optionality is [the X-bar condition] with the most effect on descriptive power of grammars', and show that not all CFLs can be weakly generated by Optionality observing grammars. From the SGC point of view, it is also obvious that imposing Optionality crucially further reduces the expressive power of SXBG, beyond what we have already discussed. For instance no grammar observing Optionality can generate a set of structural descriptions such that there is a sentence *abc* with a structural description in which occurrences $\langle a, 1\rangle$, $\langle b, 2\rangle$, $\langle c, 3\rangle$ have the constituent structure $\{\{1\}, \{2\}, \{3\}, \{1, 2, 3\}\}$ and the dependency relation $\{\langle 2, 1\rangle, \langle 3, 1\rangle\}$ but where there is no sentence *ab* with a structural description in which occurrences $\langle a, 1\rangle$, $\langle b, 2\rangle$ have the constituent structure $\{\{1\}, \{2\}, \{1, 2\}\}$ and the dependency relation $\{\langle 2, 1\rangle\}$.

Finally, to conclude our discussion of XBGs, it should be noted that the definition of the notion head proposed by Kornai and Pullum 1990 gives a less expressive definition of dependency, given its interaction with labeled constituency, than that offered by MCFGs. Kornai and Pullum propose to formalize the notion of head, as expressed in X-bar theory, in terms of a partial function h which intuitively corresponds to the notion 'labels the head daughter of'.[15] The constraints that they impose on this function, in order to simulate

[15] One of the reasons for which Kornai and Pullum suggest this formalization is that it allows the head in a local tree not to share all major syntactic features with its mother. Cf. e.g. Pullum 1991 for an application of this idea to the analysis of gerunds in English as NPs with a VP head. Note that the marking technique used in MCFGs specifies no relation whatsoever between the category of the head and the category of its mother.

X-bar theory, have as consequences that (i) each element of the V_N can only have a unique element of V_N as its head daughter; (ii) a given element of V_N can only be the head of a unique category. Thus an MCFG with rules $A \rightarrow B' \ C$ and $A \rightarrow D' \ C$ has no equivalent under their characterization since $h(A)$ would have to be either B' or D'. Similarly, an MCFG with rules $A \rightarrow B' \ C$ and $D \rightarrow B' \ E$ has no equivalent under this characterization since we would need to have $h(A) = B'$ and $h(D) = B'$. Note that in imposing these constraints Kornai and Pullum are correctly reflecting corresponding constraints of X-bar theory, which is their purpose. The constraints thus provide a characterization of the restrictions imposed by X-bar theory (as opposed to MCFGs) on the pairings of labeling interpretations and dependency relations, which we have already discussed above.

Our discussion of X-bar theory in the light of the analysis of SGC proposed here has allowed us to show clearly that Kornai and Pullum (1990: 42) were too hasty in claiming that 'maintaining the SXBG conditions commits a linguist to nothing at all as regards limits on what is describable by CFGs'. This statement is essentially true,[16] as they have shown, for most questions of WGC, but given the point of view taken here, it cannot be maintained for SGC.

4.1.5 The Expressive Power of DGs and CFGs

The above discussion may suggest that there is some sense in which CFG based grammars are inherently more expressive than DGs. This was in fact the conclusion of Gaifman 1965, comparing CFGs and DGs. As discussed above, Gaifman's result, if strictly considered relevant to CFGs, as was his original intention, is invalidated by the fact that the type of dependency interpretation that he proposes for CFGs is illegitimate. In the light of the fact that variants of CFGs can be defined in which marking constituents provides the basis for a legitimate dependency interpretation, it might appear that CFG type grammars are inherently more expressive than DGs, since they allow for a wider range of constituent structures on a string, given a certain dependency relation. However, I showed in Miller (1983: 119-121), that the nonterminal vocabulary in DGs can be marked so that it is possible for them to express the full range of constituency structures on a string definable in terms of CFGs, given a certain dependency relation on that string. This

[16] The hedge here comes from the fact that their proof requires the use of empty categories to go through in certain cases.

fact clearly shows the crucial expressive power that can be provided by marking, given the choice of appropriate Interpretation Functions, and refutes any notion that dependency based systems are inherently less expressive than phrase structure based ones.[17]

4.2 Discontinuous Constituency in Phrase Structure Grammars

4.2.1 Introduction

The variants of CFGs discussed up to here have in common that they can only express constituent structures satisfying constraints (2.4a, b, c) and (2.9) of Chapter 2, which I repeat here in (32).

(32) a. S belongs to Γ; and

b. If E_1 and E_2 belong to Γ, and the intersection of E_1 and E_2 is not empty, then :
E_1 is included in E_2; or
E_2 is included in E_1.

c. For all occurrences $\langle v, i\rangle$ belonging to S, $\{\langle v, i\rangle\}$ belongs to Γ.

d. If a structural description σ generated by a CFG is assigned an interpretation $i_o \in \mathrm{ID_O}$ by $\mathrm{IF_{CFG \to O}}$, $i_o = \{\langle x_i, i\rangle, 1 \leq i \leq n\}$, then, for every set E in Γ, $\Gamma \in \mathrm{ID_C}$ and $\Gamma = \mathrm{IF_{CFG \to C}}(\sigma)$, E is a continuous substring of i_o.

However, there have been suggestions in the linguistic literature, that constraints (32b) and (32d) should be abandoned, allowing for multidominance and discontinuous constituency respectively (cf. e.g. McCawley 1982, 1987, Higginbotham 1983, Ojeda 1987, 1988). Figures 4.15 and 4.16 illustrate these respectively.

---

[17] There is a rather clear sense in which DGs are less expressive than WMCFGs, since the latter allow partial dependency relations, but not the former. But, once again, it is easy to devise some form of marking in DGs that allows for the same partial dependency interpretations, though of course this would completely betray the intentions of those who use the DG formalism.

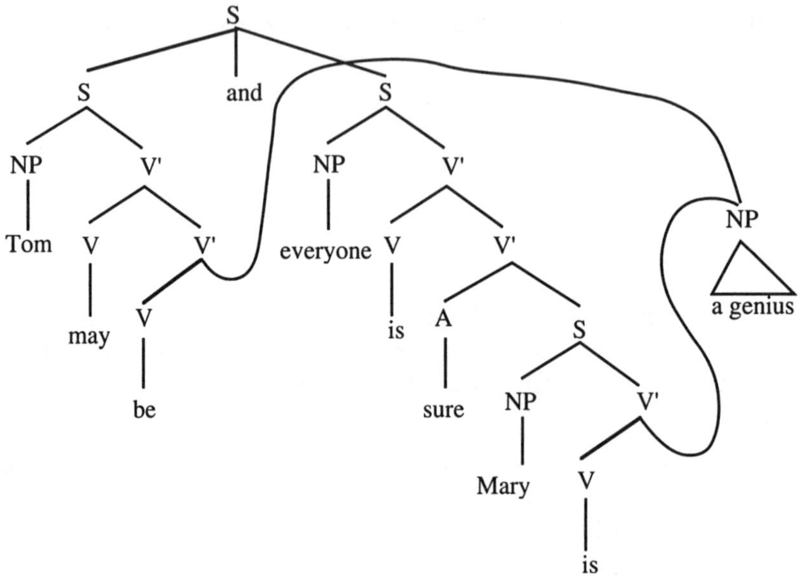

Figure 4.15

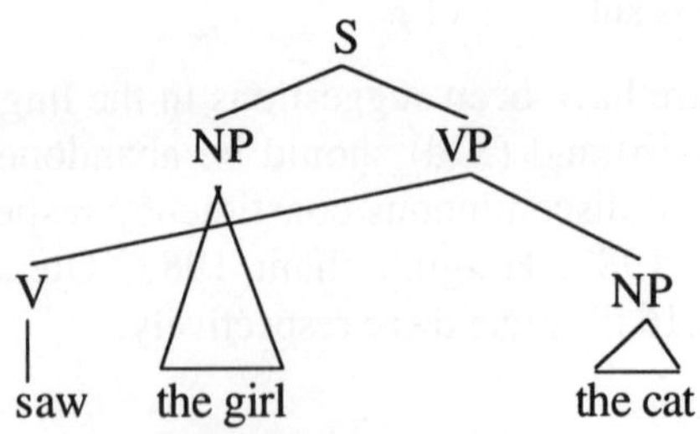

Figure 4.16

Figure 4.15, from McCawley (1982:99) illustrates the use of multidominance for the surface structure of RNR sentences. I will not discuss multidominance further here, since to my knowledge it has never been proposed as a relevant interpretation of the kinds of phrase structure systems discussed in this chapter. Figure 4.16 illustrates the kind of surface structure that one might consider for a VSO language, assuming that there is a VP constituent.[18]

Essentially, three broad classes of formalisms have been proposed to allow for discontinuous constituency, (i) the transformational formalism of McCawley 1982, 1987; (ii) the liberation systems of Pullum 1982 and Zwicky 1986; and (iii) the extension of LP constraints proposed by Ojeda 1987, 1988.

McCawley 1982, 1987 proposes a transformational grammar with a classical phrase structure base component, generating only constituent structures respecting (32a-d).[19] Some transformations, however, are assumed to change the ordering of the terminal string without changing the structural description, introducing discontinuous constituency (I will henceforth call these *reordering transformations*). For instance, the structure in Figure 4.16 would result from a deep structure like the one in Figure 4.17, by reordering of the occurrence 'saw' before the occurrences 'the girl'.

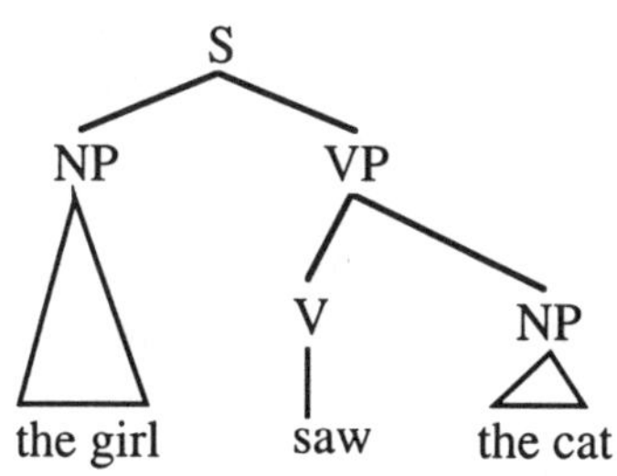

Figure 4.17

In what follows, we will discuss such transformational grammars restricting the transformations to reordering transformations, and excluding any other kind of structural change. Such grammars,

[18] Note that this is not an example that McCawley himself gives. His discussion centers on parentheticals. However, his formalism clearly allows for such an analysis.

[19] It is in fact not completely clear what McCawley 1982 assumes as the mechanism for generating deep syntactic structure (cf. his fn.3, p.94). However, he assumes that there is a relevant stage in the derivation where the structural descriptions are totally ordered and obey conditions (32). We can assume for the purposes of our discussion that such structures are directly generated by a phrase structure mechanism. For simplicity, I will refer to these as deep structures in what follows, though this is clearly not McCawley's intention.

henceforth called TGs, thus specify a single constituent structure but two orderings, which we will call the deep and surface orderings for simplicity. The deep ordering satisfies all the conditions in (32), but the surface ordering may violate condition (32d). It is thus the pairing of the latter ordering with the constituent structure that can result in discontinuous constituency.

Pullum 1982 and Zwicky 1986 propose ID phrase structure systems with 'liberation' and LP rules, which can be interpreted as defining discontinuous constituent structures (cf. also Reape 1994; see also Hoeksema 1991, Dowty 1996 for similar systems based on categorial grammar). We will call these systems liberation grammars (LGs; a formally explicit definition is given in section 4.2.2 below). The idea of liberation can informally be understood as pruning of nodes in a structure, resulting in the daughters of the pruned nodes becoming daughters of the pruned nodes' mother, and consequently sisters of the pruned nodes' sisters. This results in a new (and larger) domain over which LP rules will be applicable. For the case of VSO languages, one could generate a structure such as that in Figure 4.17, liberate the daughters of VP into S by pruning the VP node, and enforce the LP rule V $\prec$ NP among the resulting sisters (this is in fact one of the leading ideas of Pullum 1982, suggested as a way of allowing for the existence of VPs in VSO languages at some level within the general framework of PSGs). This results in the tree given in Figure 4.18.

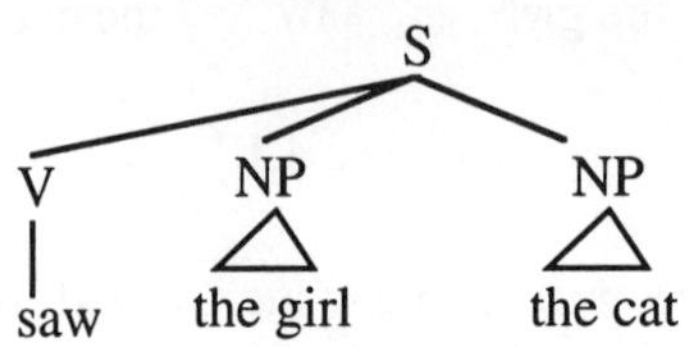

Figure 4.18

The question of the appropriate interpretations for LGs in terms of constituency and ordering is not a priori clear. Zwicky 1986 seems to assume that a derivation in an LG should define a single constituent structure and a single ordering on the string, namely that of the liberated structure. Such an interpretation can obviously be trivially obtained by choosing an appropriate Interpretation Function applying to derivations as just sketched. However, Zwicky assumes that, somehow, feature instantiation principles in the style of GKPS should be able to apply as if the non-liberated structure were accessible. Similarly, one might assume that the semantics should have access to the non-liberated structure (this is the assumption explicitly made by Dowty 1996). These intentions might be taken to indicate that structural descriptions generated by LGs should in fact define two distinct constituent structures and two orderings. The ID rules define a 'deep' constituent structure, which indirectly defines a partial ordering on the occurrences, assuming that it does not allow discontinuous constituency (this corresponds to Figure 4.17 in the preceding example). Liberation defines a 'surface' constituent structure, flatter than the deep structure, and totally ordered in a way that respects the LP rules (this corresponds to Figure 4.18 in the example). It should be clear that there is no necessary procedural intention to be derived from the use made here of the terms 'deep' and 'surface'. Obviously LGs can be defined in a procedural way, using a context-free base and pruning transformations which derive a 'liberated' surface structure. But, as is shown in section 4.2.2, it is simple to define derivations in LGs without any kind of 'liberation transformations'. LGs can be understood to define a discontinuous constituent structure if a set of occurrences forming a constituent in the deep constituent structure does not form a contiguous substring in surface constituent structure. More generally, the pairing of the deep constituent structure with the surface ordering will indicate any eventual discontinuous constituents.

Finally, Ojeda 1987, 1988 proposes a variant of ID/LP grammars as defined by GKPS, allowing LP rules to order nodes that are not sister nodes. Specifically, Ojeda proposes *partial* linear precedence rules (PLPs) of the form $\phi(A) \prec \psi(B)$, where "ϕ, ψ denote each a function from (singleton sets of) nodes N to sets of nodes dominated by N" (Ojeda 1988: 474). We will call such grammars ID/PLP grammars. For instance, Ojeda proposes the rule H(VP) $\prec$ NP (i.e. 'the head of a VP node must precede NP sisters of that VP node') to account for VSO ordering, directly assigning VSO sentences a structure like that in Figure 4.16.[20] Thus, ID/PLP grammars are like grammars with reordering transformations in that they assign a unique constituent structure to the sentence. Under their most obvious interpretation, they assign only a single (surface) ordering to a sentence, although one can legitimately obtain a 'deep' partial ordering from the constituent structure, if desired, as was just illustrated for LGs. Obviously, it is the pairing of the surface

---

[20] In fact, Ojeda (1988: 476) proposes that the head of VP must *immediately precede* an NP sister of VP, i.e. H(VP) $\prec\!\prec$ NP.

ordering with the unique constituent structure that can give rise to discontinuous constituency.

4.2.2 Liberation Grammars

Building on Zwicky 1986, we define Liberation Grammars (LGs) as follows. An LG is a 6-tuple $G = (V_N, V_T, [], P, L, S)$ where V_N is the nonterminal vocabulary; V_T is the terminal vocabulary; [] is the liberation operator, which may apply to elements of V_N. We note the application of the liberation operator to an element A of V_N as $[A]$. We use the notation $[V_N]$ to designate the set of items in V_N with the liberation operator applied to them. P is a set of productions $Q \rightarrow x$, where Q belongs either to V_N or to $[V_N]$ and where x is a multiset over $V_N \cup [V_N] \cup V_T$; L is a set of Linear Precedence (LP) statements noted $A \prec B$, where $A, B \in V_N$, forming a partial ordering (transitive and asymmetric) over V_N; finally, S is the start symbol.[21] We note strings in $(V_N \cup V_T)^*$ using σ with a subscript.

The language generated by an LG can be informally described as the set of sentences obtained as follows. Using the productions, generate a terminated ID tree. Prune all nodes to which the liberation operator applies, changing their daughters to daughters of their mother node. Order the resulting tree in any way compatible with the LP principles L.

It is possible to define the notion of derivation in an LG directly, without recourse to a procedurally defined flattening operation. Let $\sigma_i = \sigma_j\, A\, \sigma_k$, $A \in V_N$. Then, by definition, $\sigma_i \Rightarrow \sigma_{i+1}$ if and only if (i) $\sigma_{i+1} = \sigma_j\, \sigma_p\, \sigma_k$; and (ii) either (a) $A \rightarrow \sigma_p \in P$, or (b) $A \rightarrow x \in P$, where x contains at least one element of $[V_N]$, and $x \Rightarrow^*{}_{G'}\, \sigma_p$; and (iii) if σ_p is ordered such that if $\sigma_p = \sigma_u\, A\, \sigma_v\, B\, \sigma_w$, then $B \prec A \notin L$, with $A, B \in V_N$. L(LG) is then the set of strings x over V_T such that $\mathrm{S} \Rightarrow^* x$ by LG.

In (ii, b), G' is a CFG $(V_N', V_T', S\,, P)$ where $V_N' = V_N \cup [V_N]$, $V_T' = V_T$, and $P' = \{A \rightarrow z \in P \mid A \in [V_N]\}$. That is, we obtain G' from G by dropping the linearization component, collapsing the V_N with the set $[V_N]$ of applications of the liberation operator to elements of V_N (note that these items $[A]$ are atomic symbols in G'), and keeping only those productions that have an element of $[V_N]$ on the left side (i.e. the constituents to be liberated), reinterpreting them as classical ordered CF

[21] Following Zwicky 1986, we are assuming that the productions are Immediate Dominance (ID) rules in the sense of GKPS, i.e. rules that specify only dominance relations, not ordering relations. The latter are determined by the LP rules L, cf. 3.7 above.

rules, rather than ID rules. This grammar G' constructs, for each step in the derivation of G, a string σ_p which contains no occurrences of items from $[V_N]$, by developing only non-terminals belonging to $[V_N]$ and leaving those belonging to V_N untouched.

4.2.3 Comparison in SGC

Let us now compare these three systems in SGC with respect to labeled ordered constituency. We show that LGs are strictly included both in ID/PLP grammars and in TGs and that ID/PLP grammars are included in TGs (for this case it is not known whether the inclusion is strict or not).

As discussed above, all three systems can be thought of as imposing a deep constituent structure, where all constituents are continuous. This is explicitly the case in TG, and implicitly in LG and ID/PLP. All three systems also provide for a second surface ordering, which can lead to discontinuous constituency when paired with the deep constituent structure. We want to be able to characterize the range of discontinuous constituency interpretations allowed by each system in the sense of section 3.6.1.4, i.e. the range of possible pairings (Γ, O) of deep constituency and surface orderings. In fact, all three are unrestricted in this respect. They can describe the full cross product of constituent structures and orderings on sets of occurrences. For transformational grammars, it is obvious that arbitrary reordering operations can associate an arbitrary surface order with a given deep constituent structure. ID/PLP is also unrestricted: given a deep constituent structure, any surface ordering can be defined by choosing an appropriate set of PLP statements. As for LGs, it is also easy to see that they can describe any pairing (Γ, O). For any deep constituent structure, since the number of occurrences is finite, we can assign each of the atomic constituents a different label in the non-terminal vocabulary and liberate all phrasal nodes. The resulting flat surface structure can then be ordered as desired by an appropriate choice of LP rules. We have thus shown that $\mathrm{IF}_{\mathrm{TG}\rightarrow\mathrm{OC}}(\Sigma(\mathrm{TG})) = \mathrm{IF}_{\mathrm{ID/PLP}\rightarrow\mathrm{OC}}(\Sigma(\mathrm{ID/PLP})) = \mathrm{IF}_{\mathrm{LG}\rightarrow\mathrm{OC}}(\Sigma(\mathrm{LG}))$, all three being equal to the subset of $\mathrm{ID}_{\mathrm{OC}}$ for which (32a, b, c) hold.

Let us now turn to the more interesting question of the SGC of these formalisms at the level of individual grammars, rather than the level of the range of structural descriptions which can be generated by the formalisms. We first show by construction that for any LG, there is a strongly equivalent TG, with respect to ordered constituency. Take the context-free base component of the TG to be the ID rule set of the LG, with an arbitrary ordering on right hand sides of productions. We simulate the effect of an LP rule $A \prec B$ by constructing a transformation which orders A before B, if the nodes on the ascending paths from A to N and B to N are exclusively labeled with elements of $[V_N]$, where N is the lowest node dominating both A and B (N itself does not have to be labeled with an element of $[V_N]$). Obviously, the kind of structural analysis just sketched can be expressed in any classical formalization of TG (e.g. Peters and Ritchie 1973). The structural change is non-standard, since it involves creating a tree with 'crossing branches', but the intention is clear. Providing a detailed formalization is beyond the scope of this study.

Second, we can show by construction that for any LG G, there is a strongly equivalent ID/PLP grammar G' with respect to ordered constituency. Let us take the ID rules of G as the ID rules of G'. For every LP rule $A \prec B$ in G, we create a set of PLP rules in G' as follows: For every element N in $V_N \cup [V_N]$, we create the PLP rule $\phi(A, N) \prec \phi(B, N)$. We define ϕ, such that $\phi(B, N)$ is the set of nodes labeled B, dominated by N and such that the path from N to B, contains only nodes labeled with elements of $[V_N]$ (we take domination to be reflexive, so that if $N = B$, N is in $\phi(B, N)$). Thus, the PLP rules in G' simulate LP rules over liberated structures of G by a condition on paths which checks whether or not two nodes with the relevant labels would be sisters in the liberated structure of the corresponding G.

Third, we can show that inclusion of LGs in TGs is strict with respect to labeled ordered constituency. The proof here is based on the ECPO property of LGs, due to the use of LP rules. A TG can have a transformation reordering a B before an A in case there is a C between them (e.g. $A—X—C—Y—B \Rightarrow B—X—C—Y—A$). There is no way that an LG can simulate this. In order to be able to reorder As and Bs at all, with respect to the deep ordering, it has to liberate them into the same constituent. But then, it cannot differentially order them depending on whether or not there is a C in a given constituent. It is not clear that a similar reasoning can be held to show that ID/PLP grammars are strongly included in TGs with respect to labeled ordered constituency. Indeed, arbitrary functions ϕ and ψ in PLP rules could be set up so as to circumvent the ECPO constraint.

Finally, we can show that LGs are strictly included in ID/PLP grammars with respect to labeled ordered constituency. Indeed, in order to impose ordering constraints on the nodes appearing at the ends of the paths specified by the various functions ϕ, ψ, of an ID/PLP grammar, an

LG has to liberate them into a single constituent. The resulting sister nodes are ordered by LP rules, and consequently have to satisfy ECPO. This is not necessarily the case in the original ID/PLP grammar, since, given a PLP rule $\phi(A) \prec \psi(B)$ not all the nodes dominated by nodes A and B must be ordered so as to satisfy ECPO.

Thus, we have shown that with respect to labeled ordered constituency, we have the inclusion hierarchy indicated in (33a). With respect to ordered constituency without labeling, we have shown that hierarchy (33b) holds. It is not known at present whether the inclusions in the latter case are strict or not.

(33) a. TG $\supseteq$ ID/PLP $\supset$ LG
b. TG $\supseteq$ ID/PLP $\supseteq$ LG

4.3 Endocentricity

In this section, I introduce a new Interpretation Domain ID_A, for the representation of endocentricity, that is, constructions of which a subpart has the same (distributional) properties as the whole construction.[22] In such cases, the items added to the said subpart are called *adjuncts*, and such constructions are commonly referred to as *head-adjunct* structures in current transformational literature. A consequence of this distributional definition is that adjuncts can be repeated any number of times.

4.3.1 Expression of Endocentricity in CFGs

In CFGs, it is standard to interpret as adjunction structures configurations in which a mother node and one and only one of its daughters bear the same label, as in Figure 4.19, where *big* is interpreted as an adjunct to *book*.

[22] This is a classical structuralist/distributionalist notion, cf. e.g. Bloomfield 1933 §12.10, Harris 1951 §16.52fn. The Interpretation Domain for Adjunction ID_A was defined in a slightly different form in Miller 1986-7 in order to explore the string analysis model of Harris 1962, formalized by Joshi et al. 1972 as String Adjunct Grammars (SAGs), for which endocentricity is the principle interpretation. Miller 1986-7 also proposed an Interpretation Function for Adjunction applicable to CFGs, and showed that CFGs are more powerful than SAGs in this respect. That paper also showed that SAGs are strictly included in CFGs wrt constituency interpretations.

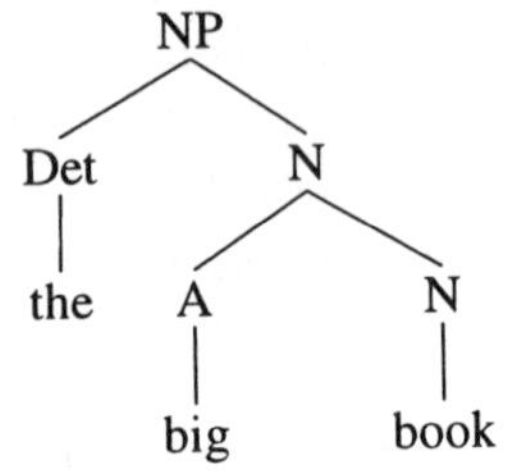

Figure 4.19

Note that, in the general case, sets of occurrences can be specified by CFGs to be adjoined to sets of occurrences (rather than single occurrences to single occurrences as in the example). This is the case, for instance, under classical (though not uncontroversial) assumptions according to which instrumental PPs are adjoined to VP, as in (34).

(34) Kim [$_{\text{VP}}$ [$_{\text{VP}}$ opened the door] [$_{\text{PP}}$ with a key]].

In this case, we want to be able to express the idea that the occurrences *with a key* are adjoined to the occurrences *opened the door*. To do this, we can say that the pair ⟨{*with*, *a*, *key*}, {*opened*, *the*, *door*}⟩ is in the *adjunct structure* of (34).[23]

More generally, let us define an adjunct structure as a set of pairs, where the first member is a set of sets of occurrences, and the second is a set of occurrences. If $\langle\{M_1, ..., M_m\}, N\rangle$ is such a pair in an adjunct structure, we take this to mean that the sets of occurrences M_i, $1 \leq i \leq m$, are adjoined to the set of occurrences N. Taking into account the idea that there can be more than one set of occurrences adjoined to another, we revise the adjunct analysis of (34) to {⟨{{*with*, *a*, *key*}}, {*opened*, *the*, *door*}⟩}. Obviously, the definition of adjunction presented here has as a consequence that any adjunct structure implicitly defines a constituent structure. This constitutes further evidence in favor of the centrality of constituent structure interpretations in linguistics.

We can then define the Interpretation Domain for adjunction, ID_A, as the set of adjunct structures. The following Interpretation Function

[23] I am using terminals here, rather than occurrences of terminals, for notational simplicity, taking advantage of the fact that none of the terminals occur twice in the example.

will map structural descriptions generated by CFGs to their classically assumed intended interpretation $\mathcal{A}$ in $\mathrm{ID_A}$.[24]

(35) $\mathrm{IF_{CFG \to A}} : \Sigma(\mathrm{CFG}) \to \mathrm{ID_A}$: $\sigma \to \mathcal{A}$, such that for every local tree in σ where the mother is labeled A and one and only one daughter is labeled A, and the other daughters are labeled $B_1, ..., B_m$, the pair $\langle\{M_1, ..., M_m\}, N\rangle$ belongs to $\mathcal{A}$, where M_i is the set of occurrences dominated by B_i, $1 \leq i \leq m$, and N is the set of occurrences dominated by A.

Let us consider what range of interpretations in $\mathrm{ID_A}$ can be represented by derivations in CFGs, that is, what array of properties characterizes $\mathrm{IF_{CFG \to A}}(\Sigma(\mathrm{CFG}))$. In this respect it should be noted that, because of the way the Interpretation Function $\mathrm{IF_{CFG \to A}}$ is set up, we can be sure that (a) all the sets $M_1, ..., M_m, N$ in an element of an adjunct structure are constituents; (b) they are disjoint; (c) their union is a constituent. Furthermore, the constituent N bears the same label as the constituent which is the union of $M_1, ..., M_m, N$. These properties express the main restrictions on the compatibility of adjunct structure, constituent structure and labeling in CFGs. On this basis, we can characterize the necessary and sufficient conditions on adjunct structures so that they can be represented by a structural description in a CFG, i.e. (36) characterizes $\mathrm{IF_{CFG \to A}}(\Sigma(\mathrm{CFG}))$.

---

24 This choice of Interpretation Function leads us to distinguish the adjunct structure of the derivations in (i) and (ii). In (i), $\{b\}$ is adjoined to $\{a\}$, and $\{c\}$ to $\{a, b\}$, whereas in (ii), both $\{b\}$ and $\{c\}$ are simply adjoined to $\{a\}$.

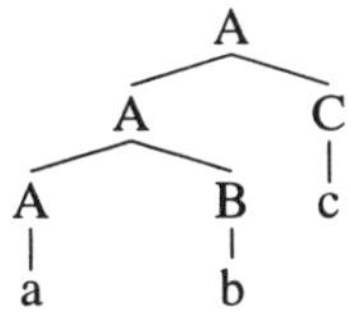

(i)

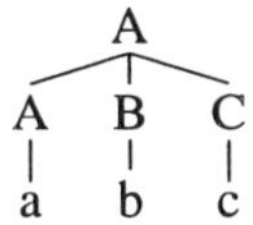

(ii)

This seems to be the natural default assumption, but under certain auxiliary hypotheses, e.g. binary branching, one might want to consider a structure like (i) as expressing that both $\{b\}$ and $\{c\}$ are adjoined to $\{a\}$. I will not explore this possibility further here, though there appears to be no problem in providing an alternate Interpretation Function giving such results.

(36) $\{\langle\{M^1{}_1, ..., M^1{}_{m_1}\}, N^1\rangle, \langle\{M^2{}_1, ..., M^2{}_{m_2}\}, N^2\rangle, ..., \langle\{M^n{}_1, ..., M^n{}_{m_n}\}, N^n\rangle\}$, is the adjunct structure of a derivation σ in a CFG if and only if $\forall\, p, q, 1 \le p, q \le n, \forall\, i, j, 1 \le i, j \le m_p$,

a. the sets $M^p{}_i$ and N^p are all continuous substrings of the terminal string of σ; and

b. the sets $M^p{}_i$ and N^p are all disjoint; and

c. the set of occurrences $M^p{}_1 \cup ... \cup M^p{}_{m_p} \cup N^p$ is a continuous substring of the terminal string of σ; and

d. if a set E appears as $M^p{}_i$ or N^p in an element of the adjunct structure, then no superset E' of E can appear as $M^q{}_j$ or N^q in another element of the adjunct structure unless E' includes all of the occurrences $M^p{}_1 \cup ... \cup M^p{}_{m_p} \cup N^p$.

It is obvious that any adjunct structure expressed by a derivation in a CFG will satisfy the conditions (36). It is also easy to show by construction that these conditions are sufficient to allow one to construct a CFG generating a derivation expressing any adjunct structure that satisfies them.

To conclude this discussion of endocentricity as expressed by CFGs, let us state the following necessary property of sets of adjunct structures expressed by individual CFGs. Let G be a CFG and let $\mathrm{IF}_{\mathrm{CFG}\rightarrow\mathrm{A}}(\Sigma(G)) = \Pi = \{\pi_1, ..., \pi_n\}$ be the set of adjunct structures expressed by G.

(37) For all G, if there is a derivation $\sigma_i \in \Sigma(G)$ where π_i is the adjunct structure defined by σ_i, and if $\langle\{M_1, ..., M_m\}, N\rangle \in \pi_i$, then (i) $M_1 \cup ... \cup M_m \cup N$, is a string of occurrences with yield $\psi_1\phi\psi_2$, ϕ being the yield of N and (ii) the yield of σ_i is of the form $\alpha\psi_1\phi\psi_2\beta$, and (iii) for each string of the type $\alpha(\psi_1)^p\phi(\psi_2)^p\beta$, $p \ge 0$, there is a derivation σ_j in $\Sigma(G)$ which has this string as its yield.

This theorem shows how our choice of Interpretation Function for adjunction for CFGs captures the intuitive notion of endocentricity, i.e. that adjuncts are repeatable.

4.3.2 Expression of Endocentricity in MCFGs

With a slight adjustment to deal with marking, the Interpretation Function for adjunction $\mathrm{IF}_{\mathrm{CFG}\rightarrow\mathrm{A}}$ will give appropriate results for the various types of MCFGs discussed in section 4.1. We want $\mathrm{IF}_{\mathrm{CFG}\rightarrow\mathrm{A}}$ to consider as relevant for identity of labeling in mother-daughter configurations only the first member of the pairs labeling nodes in

MCFG derivations. This is necessary if we want to be able to capture the intuitively obvious relation between adjunction and dependency, namely that something which is adjoined depends on that to which it is adjoined and, at the same time, to allow adjunction to nonheads (adjunction to heads does not raise these problems). Consider for instance the structure in Figure 4.20.

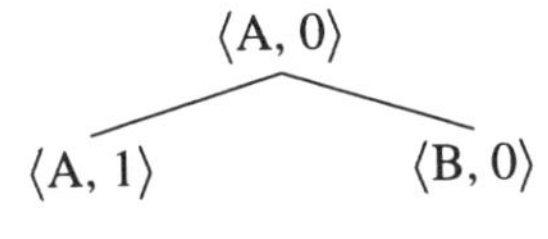

Figure 4.20

In this structure, either one of the daughters must be marked. If we chose to mark the *B* daughter, contrary to what is shown in Figure 4.20, then the labels of the mother and the *A* daughter would be strictly identical, and we would have an adjunction structure, but we would be claiming that the adjunct *B* is the head daughter. If we mark the *A* daughter, as shown, then it is the head daughter as desired, but the labels of that daughter and the mother will no longer be strictly identical. Identity will obtain only if we consider only the first member of the labeling pair to be relevant for the definition of an adjunct structure.[25]

Beyond this technicality, we want to claim that in general, adjuncts are dependents. Specifically, we require that if $\langle\{M_1, ..., M_m\}, N\rangle$ is in the adjunct structure for a given structural description, then, for all i, $1 \leq i \leq m$, the head of the M_i must depend on the head of N. Thus, the constituents M_i must bear unmarked labels and must have N as their marked sister. This constraint imposes obvious restrictions on the possible triplets of labeled constituency, dependency and endocentricity interpretations expressible by MCFGs.

25 This discussion shows why adopting the alternative definition for MCFGs discussed in section 4.1.3 above makes it impossible to define adjunction to non-heads, if adjuncts are necessarily to be interpreted as dependents. Indeed, under that definition, there are two vocabularies $V_N{}^{\circ}$ and $V_N{}'$ of atomic nonterminals, labeling non-head and head constituents respectively and consequently a non-head constituent cannot have the same label as its head daughter.

4.3.3 Expression of Endocentricity by XBGs

XBGs can be interpreted for adjunction by the Interpretation Function $IF_{CFG \rightarrow A}$, adopting a similar constraint on the link between dependency and endocentricity as that expressed above for MCFG, i.e. that an adjunct depends on that to which it is adjoined. Contrary to what was the case for MCFGs, we do not want to modify this $IF_{CFG \rightarrow A}$ so that it does not take bar level into account. Indeed, structures where the head daughter does not have the same bar level as the mother are not interpreted as adjunct structures in XBG. It should be noted, however, that if strict Succession is imposed, it will never be the case that a daughter has the same label as its mother, and no adjunction will be expressed at all.[26] Weak Succession, however, allows for adjunction, and this is in fact one of the major reasons why it is usually chosen over Strict Succession.

Note on the other hand, that if Optionality is assumed, then we want to claim that all dependents are adjuncts. Indeed, assuming Optionality is essentially equivalent to claiming that all constructions are endocentric. This leads us to a quite different way of interpreting XBG derivations in terms of adjunction, and requires an entirely different Interpretation Function, namely one which maps a structural description to an adjunct structure such that all non-head constituents are adjoined to the head constituent. This idea leads to a much more restricted range of interpretations than for CFGs or MCFGs (or XBGs without Optionality). Indeed, it is no longer possible to express exocentricity at all, and for every constituent that has subconstituents, all of the subconstituents except one are adjoined to that one.

4.3.4 A Note on Adjunction and Rule Schemata with Kleene Stars in CFGs

Infinite rule schemata of type (38a), or more generally rule schemata subsumed under (38b), where π is an arbitrary permutation operator, have sometimes been suggested in phrase structure grammars.

(38) a. $A \rightarrow B\ C^*$

b. $A \rightarrow \pi(B_1, ..., B_m, C_1^*, ...C_n^*)$

---

26 In fact, this can happen, e.g. in a case like $[_{N^2}\ [_{N^1}\ ]\ [_{N^2}\ ]]$, but given the constraint linking adjunction and dependency, this should not be interpreted as an adjunct structure since the embedded N^2 could not be the head of the whole construction, if generated by a grammar respecting strict succession.

Such usage of the Kleene star on the right hand side of a CFG production is known not to increase the WGC beyond that of standard CFGs (cf. Langendoen 1976). Rule schemata of this type might be considered to express that those elements bearing a Kleene star are adjuncts. Indeed such a rule, by its very form, implicitly states that they can be repeated any number of times in the construction. Note however that the theory of SGC presented here, where interpretation is restricted to sets of structural descriptions, makes such an interpretation illegitimate for CFGs with these types of rules. Indeed, consider the form of the derivations generated, shown in Figure 4.21.

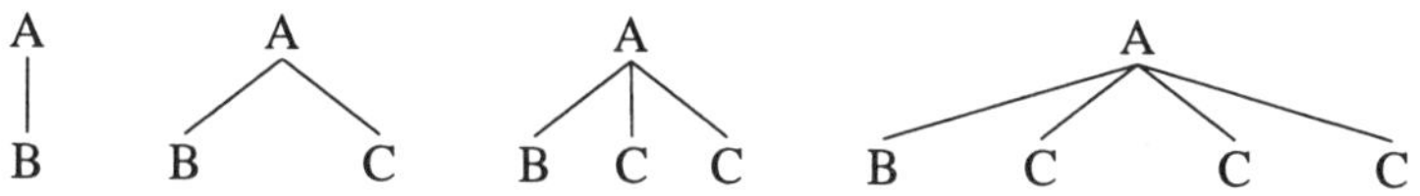

Figure 4.21

Obviously, there is no way that an Interpretation Function could distinguish the status of any of these structures, generated by rule (38a), from that of identical structures generated by rules $A \rightarrow B$, $A \rightarrow B\ C$, $A \rightarrow B\ C\ C$, $A \rightarrow B\ C\ C\ C$ in grammars without (38a). But in such grammars, these structures would not have an intended interpretation in terms of adjunction. It is only by interpreting the rule system directly that one could capture the difference. But, I have argued at length that the idea of interpreting grammars directly, rather than the structural derivations they generate, leads to insuperable difficulties. The question arises then of whether there is any way that we can somehow make minor adjustments to the nature of the structural descriptions generated by such grammars so that we can get a legitimate interpretation of the kind desired. In this respect, it is useful to compare the situation here with that discussed for ordering in ID/LP grammars, in section 4.2.1. The main difference between the two cases is that the desired interpretation, ordering, is directly represented in the derivation in the case of ID/LP grammars, by the order of branches in the tree, in a way that adjunct status is not. Thus, the obvious solution to the problem at hand is to directly represent adjunct status in structural descriptions. To do this, we can simply use an alternative form of marking, beyond that used for dependency, for instance marking adjuncts with a special feature °, (or inversely marking the endocentric head with a special feature). Either we modify the definition of production, so that elements marked with the Kleene star on right hand sides of productions have to bear this feature, or we modify the definition of structural description, so that nodes in structures corresponding to elements bearing a Kleene star are marked with this feature. Under either of these approaches, we get the structures in Figure 4.22, instead of the ones in Figure 4.21.

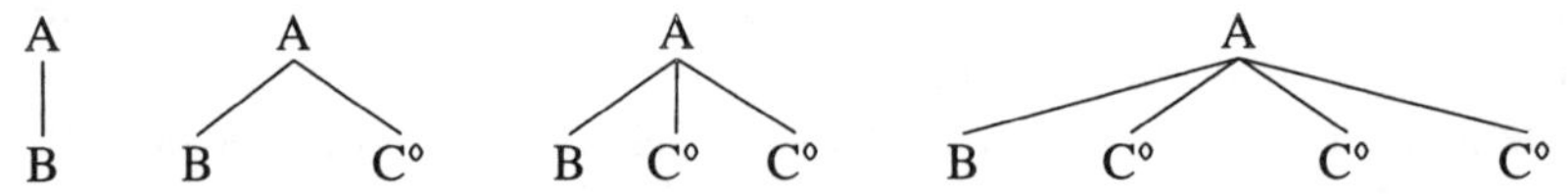

Figure 4.22

These structures obviously allow for a legitimate interpretation in terms of endocentricity. Furthermore, contrary to the approach discussed above in section 4.3.1, these types of rules force all adjuncts to a head to be attached as sisters to that head, and do not allow them to appear higher, because of the fact that the head of the endocentric construction (*B* in these examples) can be of a different category than the whole construction (*A* in the examples).

Chapter 5

Aspects of the Strong Generative Capacity of Categorial Grammars

5.1 Legitimate Interpretations of Simple Categorial Grammars

5.1.1 Simple Categorial Grammars

A Categorial Grammar (CG)[1] can be defined as a 6-tuple $\langle BC, D, R, V_T, A, S \rangle$, where *BC* is a set of basic categories; *D* is a set of rules for deriving the set of categories *C*; *R* is a set of reduction rules; V_T is the terminal vocabulary and *A* is an assignment relation between V_T and *C*, assigning each lexical element to one or more (basic or complex) categories. Different classes of CGs can be defined based on the choice of *D* and of *R*. For simple CGs (also known as *Bar-Hillel CGs*), we take *D* to be defined as in (1) and *R* to include the single rule (2), known as function application. In (2), $(X_1 \ldots X_{i-1} \backslash X_i / X_{i+1} \ldots X_n)$ is the *functor* category and $X_1, \ldots X_{i-1}, X_{i+1}, \ldots X_n$, are the *argument* categories.[2] Various forms of Generalized CGs can be obtained by varying the rules *R*, either by adding rules on a piecemeal basis (as done e.g. by Steedman 1985), or by deriving them as theorems of a more general logic of types, e.g. the Lambek calculus (cf. e.g. Moortgat 1989, Desclés 1990 for a general discussion).

---

[1] The systems discussed here have their origin in Ajdukiewicz 1935. They were first compared in WGC with CFGs by Bar-Hillel et al. 1964. See Moortgat 1989 for a general discussion of CG and references.

[2] I am adopting the notations of Moortgat 1989 for complex categories, with arguments systematically under the fraction sign, rather than those of e.g. Steedman 1985, in which arguments are systematically to the right of the fraction sign. By convention, upper case letters from the beginning of the roman alphabet (*A*, *B*, ...) designate basic categories, and upper case letters from the end of the alphabet (*X*, *Y*, ...) designate categories, basic or complex.

(1) a. If a category B belongs to BC, then B belongs to C.
b. If categories $X_1, ..., X_n$ belong to C, then $(X_1 \ldots X_{i\text{-}1} \backslash X_i / X_{i+1} \ldots X_n)$ belongs to C, $1 \leq i \leq n$.

(2) $X_1 \ldots X_{i\text{-}1} \quad (X_1 \ldots X_{i\text{-}1} \backslash X_i / X_{i+1} \ldots X_n) \quad X_{i+1} \ldots X_n \Rightarrow X_i$, $1 \leq i \leq n$.

Figures 5.1 and 5.2 give examples of structural descriptions derived in such grammars. Note the possibility, provided by (1) and (2), of combining more than two constituents at one time as illustrated in Figure 5.2, allowing for a 'flat' structure.[3]

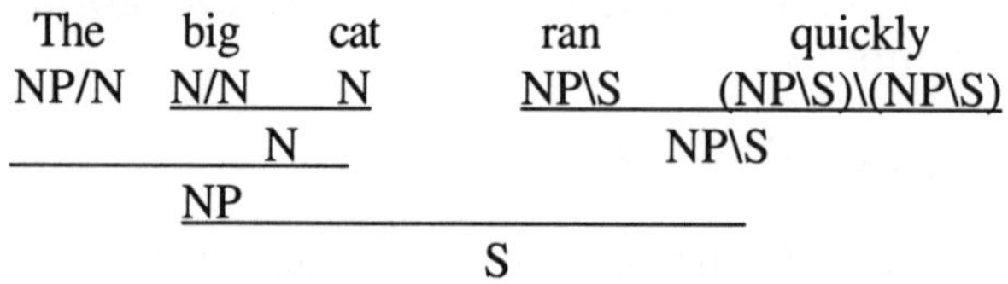

Figure 5.1

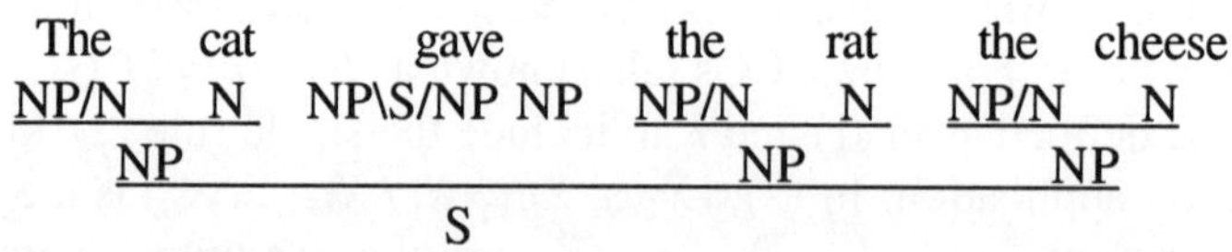

Figure 5.2

5.1.2 Constituency and Labeling

Simple categorial grammars have an obvious interpretation in terms of constituency. The Interpretation Function for simple CGs for constituency, $IF_{CG \to C}$, can be stated in the obvious way.

---

[3] This possibility, which is present in the definition of Bar-Hillel et al. 1964, is often neglected, with reduction rules being limited to binary reductions. It is crucial to the discussion below of the expressive power of simple CG with respect to constituency.

(3) $IF_{CG \rightarrow C} : \Sigma(CG) \rightarrow ID_C : \sigma \rightarrow \Gamma$ such that
   a. each occurrence in σ is a constituent in Γ;
   b. the constituent corresponding to the lexical categories is the singleton occurrence with which it is associated;
   c. for each instance of function application in σ, the union of the constituents corresponding to the categories involved forms a constituent in Γ, corresponding to the resulting category.

For Figure 5.1, this gives us constituent structure (4) (omitting indices).

(4) {{the}, {big}, {cat}, {ran}, {quickly}, {big, cat}, {ran, quickly}, {the, big, cat}, {the, big, cat, ran, quickly}}

It is also possible to define an interpretation for CGs in terms of labeled constituent structure. The obvious choice is to label constituents by the category associated with them in the derivation. Given the role of the categories in the derivation, it is clear that the possible choices of a labeling interpretation given a choice of constituency on a string, will be restricted in ways that are not paralleled in e.g. CFGs.

More complex conceptions of labeling are potentially desirable. For instance, Dowty 1996 implicitly assumes a double labeling of constituents. Indeed, he formulates LP rules for ordering derivations in CG on the basis of classical phrase structure grammar style category labels, e.g. NP, PP, VP, etc. Such an analysis requires adding a component to simple CG, responsible for assigning such PSG style labels appropriately, given the usual categorially based labeling, and could lead to setting up an Interpretation Domain where constituent structures are associated with a pair of labelings.

5.1.3 Endocentricity

There is an obvious and classical way to interpret derivations in a simple CG in terms of endocentricity. We will interpret instances of binary function application where the category of the argument is the same as that of the result as endocentric constructions where the functor is adjoined to the argument. This occurs if the functor is of type *X/X* or *X\X* and the argument of type *X*. Indeed, in such cases, the formalism allows the functor to be repeated any number of times as illustrated in Figures 5.3a, 5.3b, and 5.3c.[4]

---

[4] This is a classical idea, cf. e.g. Moortgat (1989: 6). Note however that a more liberal interpretation of adjunction is possible. We could consider that any instance of function application where one and only one of the categories involved is identical to

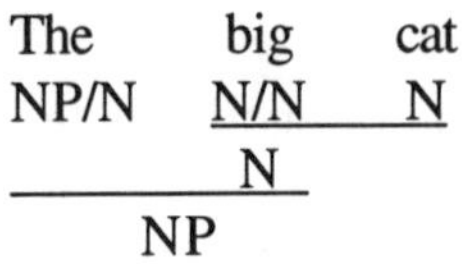

Figure 5.3a

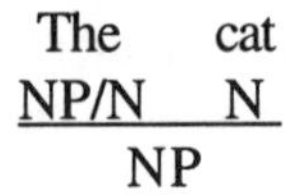

Figure 5.3b

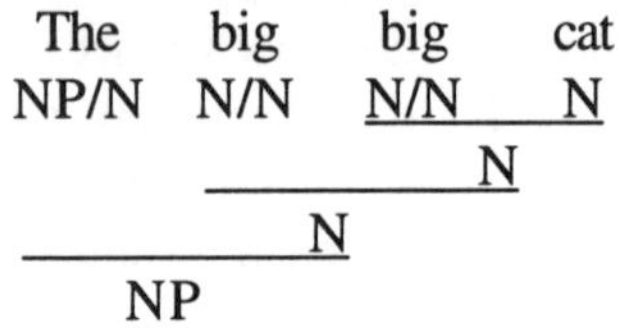

Figure 5.3c

The Interpretation Function in (5) will ensure that we get the appropriate results for structures like these (the notion of correspondence used here is the one defined in (3) above). (6) gives the adjunct structure corresponding to Figure 5.3c.[5]

(5) $IF_{CG \to A} : \Sigma(CG) \to ID_A : \sigma \to \mathcal{A}$ such that for all instances of function application in σ, if the functor is of type X/X or $X\backslash X$ and the argument is of type X, the pair $\langle \{E\}, E' \rangle$ is in the adjunct structure $\mathcal{A}$, where E is the set of occurrences corresponding to the functor and E' is the set of occurrences corresponding to the argument.

(6) $\{\langle\{\{\langle \text{big}, 3\rangle\}\}, \{\langle \text{cat}, 4\rangle\}\rangle, \langle\{\{\langle \text{big}, 2\rangle\}\}, \{\langle \text{big}, 3\rangle, \langle \text{cat}, 4\rangle\}\rangle\}$

Clearly, given the restriction of adjunction interpretations to binary branching structures, pairs $\langle \{E\}, E' \rangle$ in adjunct structures will always have a singleton as their first member.[6]

5.1.4 Functor-Argument Structure

Simple CGs allow for an obvious interpretation in terms of functor-argument structure. This interpretation is even more crucial for generalized CG. We can define a functor-argument structure $\mathcal{F}$ as a set of pairs $\langle S_1, \{S_2, ..., S_n\}\rangle$, $n \geq 2$. The first item in the pair is a set of

---

the result is a case of adjunction of all the other sister categories to the one identical to the resulting category. I will not explore this possibility further, since it does not appear to have been suggested by users of CG.

[5] Indices are included in (6) to distinguish occurrences of 'big'.

[6] There is an alternative way of interpreting derivations in CGs, parallel to the one suggested in fn.24 of section 4.3.1 for CFGs, which permits one to overcome this restriction. Namely, interpreting a structure like the one in Figure 5.3c as expressing the adjunct structure $\{\langle\{\{\langle \text{big}, 2\rangle\}, \{\langle \text{big}, 3\rangle\}\}, \{\langle \text{cat}, 4\rangle\}\rangle\}$, where both occurrences of *big* are adjoined to the head *cat*.

occurrences. The second is a set of sets of occurrences. The presence of such a pair in the functor-argument structure indicates that the sets of occurrences S_2, ..., S_n are arguments of the set of occurrences S_1, i.e. that the constituents S_2, ..., S_n are arguments of the constituent S_1 (this shows yet again the centrality of constituent structure interpretations; once again they are an automatic by-product of another interpretation). We can then define the Interpretation Domain for functor-argument structures, $\mathrm{ID_{FA}}$, as the set of all such sets of pairs. The Interpretation Function $\mathrm{IF_{CG \rightarrow FA}}$ in (7) will map structural descriptions in simple CGs to their intended interpretation in $\mathrm{ID_{FA}}$.

(7) $\mathrm{IF_{CG \rightarrow FA}} : \Sigma(\mathrm{CG}) \rightarrow \mathrm{ID_{FA}} : \sigma \rightarrow \mathcal{F}$ such that for each instance of function application of a functor to n arguments in σ, there is a pair in the functor-argument structure $\mathcal{F}$, the first item of which contains all of the occurrences corresponding to the functor, and the second item of which is the set of sets of occurrences corresponding to each of the arguments.

This Interpretation Function will assign the functor-argument structure $\mathcal{F}_1$ in (8a) to the structural description given in Figure 5.1 above, and $\mathcal{F}_2$ in (8b) to Figure 5.2 (ignoring indices for perspicuity).

(8) a. $\mathcal{F}_1$ = {⟨{big}, {{cat}}⟩, ⟨{quickly}, {{ran}}⟩, ⟨{the}, {{big, cat}}⟩, ⟨{ran, quickly}, {{the, big, cat}}⟩}
b. $\mathcal{F}_2$ = {⟨{the}, {{cat}}⟩, ⟨{the}, {{rat}}⟩, ⟨{the}, {{cheese}}⟩, ⟨{gave}, {{the, cat}, {the, rat}, {the, cheese}}⟩}

Note that for any derivation, there will be one and only one occurrence which is never included in the arguments of its functor-argument structure (that is, in the sets appearing in the second element of the pairs). In the case of Figure 5.1, this is *quickly* and in Figure 5.2, *gave*. We will call this occurrence the *main functor*.

5.1.5 Dependency

There are two obvious ways to define dependency in simple CGs, given in (9) and (10). The former, provided by the Interpretation Function $\mathrm{IF_{CG \rightarrow ID}}$, essentially identifies the dependency relation with the functor-argument structure, assigning the heads of the arguments as dependents of the heads of the functor. In this case, the independent occurrence is simply identified with the main functor occurrence. However, this position results in a conflict with the classical interpretation for endocentricity just discussed, since an adjunct is then identified as the head in the dependency relation. The second Interpretation Function $IF_{CG \rightarrow 2D}$, given in (10), which we will be using unless otherwise specified, overcomes this difficulty by explicitly distinguishing the status of adjuncts, in a way that is classical in CG thinking (cf. e.g. Moortgat 1989: 6). It assigns dependent status to the optional item in endocentric constructions.[7]

(9) $IF_{CG \rightarrow 1D} : \Sigma(CG) \rightarrow ID_D : \sigma \rightarrow R$ such that for instances of functional application in σ, the occurrences corresponding to the heads of the arguments are dependent on the occurrence corresponding to the head of the functor.

(10) $IF_{CG \rightarrow 2D} : \Sigma(CG) \rightarrow ID_D : \sigma \rightarrow R$ such that for instances of functional application in σ, the occurrences corresponding to the heads of the arguments are dependent on the occurrence corresponding to the head of the functor, except if the functor is of form X/X or $X\backslash X$, and there is a unique argument of the form X, in which case the opposite is the case.

$IF_{CG \rightarrow 1D}$ and $IF_{CG \rightarrow 2D}$ respectively give us the dependency systems above and below the occurrences in (11), when applied to the structure in Figure 5.1 above.

(11) 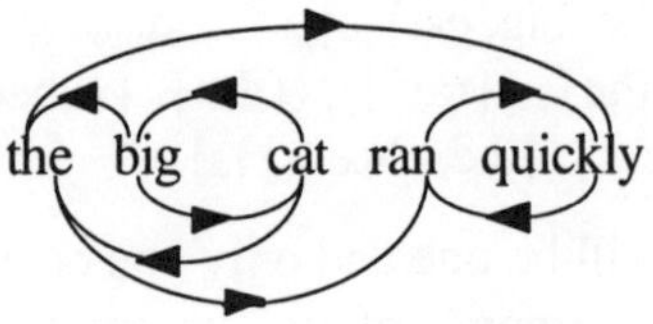

5.2 The SGC of Simple Categorial Grammars

Steedman 1985 states a commonly held view when he claims of the derivations obtained in CGs by the use of the function application rule $X/Y\ Y \Rightarrow X$ that "such diagrams are in every way equivalent to the more familiar trees associated with PS grammars", (Steedman 1985: 528). This section, in which I discuss the expressive power of simple CGs, and compare it to that of phrase structure systems, shows that such

---

[7] One can probably attribute the statement "a categorial grammar can thus give adequate representation of either endocentricity or dependence, but not both at the same time" (Levelt 1974: 100) to an intuitive reluctance towards adopting an interpretation scheme like (10) with a seemingly ad hoc exception clause.

statements are untenable given an appropriate framework for the analysis of grammatical formalisms.

5.2.1 Constituency

The following central theorems can be proved about the SGC of simple categorial grammars with respect to constituency.

(12) a. Simple CGs are strictly included in SGC in CFGs with respect to constituency.

b. A CFG G has a strongly equivalent simple CG G' with respect to constituency iff $\Sigma(G)$ is such that there is a finite bound on the length of the shortest path from occurrences of non-terminals to the terminal string.

c. The class of XBGs respecting the Maximality, Lexicality and Succession conditions of Kornai and Pullum 1990 is strongly equivalent to simple CGs with respect to constituency.

d. The class of XBGs not respecting Succession strictly includes simple CGs in SGC with respect to constituency.

e. The class of DGs and of SMCFGs are strictly included in simple CGs with respect to constituency.

To prove (12a), we first prove by construction that for every simple CG G there is a CFG G' which is strongly equivalent with respect to constituency. We then prove that inclusion is indeed strict by showing that there are CFGs for which there is no equivalent simple CG, with respect to constituency. In fact, we prove the stronger result given in (12b). The latter has (12c) as an obvious consequence, as well as (12d). Finally, (12e) is obviously true, given (12c) and (4.28a,b) of chapter 4.

Proof of (12a)

I. Construction for a CG G of a strongly equivalent CFG G' with respect to constituency.

Let W be the subset of C that contains all of the categories assigned by A to elements of V_T in G, and all of the basic and intermediate categories required to construct these categories by the rules D. We take W as the nonterminal vocabulary of G'. We define P of G' as in (13).

(13) $\forall\ (X_1 \ldots X_{i-1} \backslash X_i / X_{i+1} \ldots X_n) \in W,$
$X_i \rightarrow X_1 \ldots X_{i-1}\ (X_1 \ldots X_{i-1} \backslash X_i / X_{i+1} \ldots X_n)\ X_{i+1} \ldots X_n \in P.$

It is obvious that there is a bijective mapping between the derivation sets of G and G' which preserves constituency, and that these grammars are consequently strongly equivalent with respect to that interpretation.

II. To prove that the inclusion is strict as stated in (12a), simply consider the CFG G with productions $S \to SS$ and $S \to a$. There is no simple CG G' which can generate $L(G) = a^n$ assigning all of the possible constituent structures that G assigns. To see why this is the case, note first that function application in a simple CG always reduces complexity (defined as the number of occurrences of the connectives /, \ in a category), that is, the resulting category always contains less occurrences of the connectives than the functor category. Consequently, in the derivation set of a CG, there is a finite bound $m+1$ on the length of the paths from the root to the category directly dominating the main functor lexical item, where m is the complexity of the most complex category assigned to an element of V_T by the assignment relation A. Obviously, there is no such finite bound on the paths from the root to any preterminal item in the string in the derivation set of the above CFG G. This completes the proof of (12a).■

PROOF OF (12b)

Let us now turn to (12b). The constraint just exhibited on paths from root to main functor in simple CGs is in fact a special case of the following more general constraint. For any node in a derivation in a CG, if the category labeling the node is of complexity k, and the maximally complex category assigned to a lexical item is of complexity m, then there is a path of length smaller or equal to $(m-k)+1$ from that node to a preterminal category. Obviously, the complexity of the category labeling any node in the derivation must be smaller or equal to m. Consequently, for any node in the tree there is a finite bound $m+1$ on the length of the shortest path to the terminal string, determined by maximal complexity of lexically assigned categories.[8] This proves half of (12b), i.e. that a CFG has a strongly equivalent CG only if its derivation set is such that there is a finite bound on the length of the shortest path from occurrences of non-terminals to the terminal string. ■

---

[8] Note that these results are directly related to the impossibility of lexicalizing CFGs, discussed by Joshi and Schabes 1992.

We now prove by construction that there always is such a CG. In fact, we will prove the equivalent theorem (14).[9] This theorem is equivalent, because from any CFG satisfying the constraint in (12b), we can construct an MCFG which defines the same tree set, except that for each nonterminal in the trees we mark the nodes of one of the bounded paths from it to the terminal string. Obviously, the resulting MCFG has a finite bound on head paths.

(14) For every MCFG *G*, such that there is a finite bound on head paths, there is a strongly equivalent CG *G′* with respect to constituency.

In order to prove this theorem, we use the auxiliary concept *spine* of section 4.1.3, illustrated in Figure 5.4.

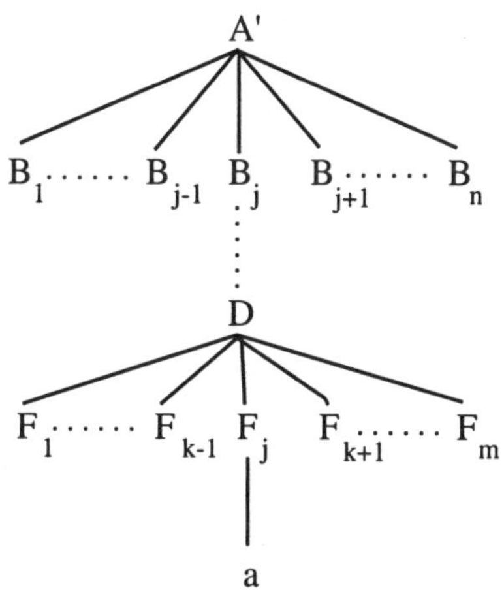

Figure 5.4

Construction of *G′*

By hypothesis, for every element *A′* in V_N', there is a finite bound on head paths rooted in *A′*. Consequently, there is a finite set HP(*A′*) of such paths for each *A′*, and a finite set SP(*A′*) of corresponding spines,

[9] Note that for the proof to go through, if we accept CFGs with syncategorematic terminals, we must adopt (2.5) of chapter 2 as the Interpretation Function for constituency for CFGs. This is because in CGs, given the definitions in section 5.1.2, each occurrence is necessarily a constituent.

of the type shown in Figure 5.4. We construct the assignment relation A of G' by assigning a category of type (15) to each terminal a that can be inserted below the preterminal (i.e. lowest) head node of each head path of the type shown in Figure 5.4.

(15) $F_1...F_k\backslash(...\backslash(B_1...B_j\backslash A'/B_{j+1}...B_n)/...)/F_{k+1}...F_m$

Furthermore, for all productions $B \rightarrow b$ in P, where $B \in V_N$, we assign the lexical item b the category B by the assignment relation A in G'. This definition of the assignment relation A induces a *CG* G' strongly equivalent to G with respect to constituency, completing our proof of (14), and therefore of (12b). ■

PROOF OF (12c)

Clearly, as discussed in section 4.1.4, SXBGs, which respect (Strict) Succession, have derivation trees such that for each nonterminal with bar-level n, the shortest path to a terminal is of length n+1 (this will always be the path to the head). Consequently, there will always be a strongly equivalent CG with respect to constituency. On the other hand, because of the bound on paths from nodes in derivations to the terminal string in CGs, it is always possible to construct an equivalent XBG with respect to constituency. ■

Note that imposing Maximality and/or Uniformity does not weaken XBGs with respect to constituency, because the non-branching local trees that need to be added to derivations to satisfy these conditions do not change the constituency properties of the derivations, as illustrated in Figures 5.5a,b,c (i.e. even if you add V' to Figure 5.5a, giving 5.5b, the result still expresses the same constituent structure as 5.5c).

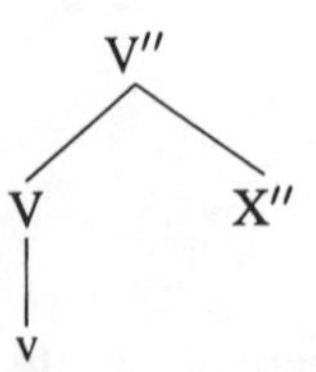

Figure 5.5a

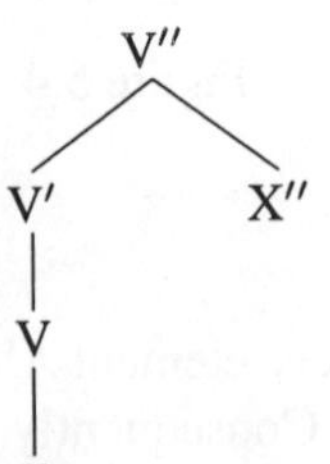

Figure 5.5b

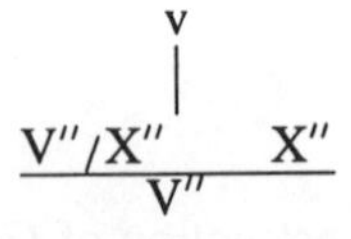

Figure 5.5c

Finally, (12d) is obvious since relaxing Succession makes it possible to obtain derivations in XBGs which violate the necessary condition on bounded paths to the terminal string of (12b)

5.2.2 Dependency

The expressive power of simple CGs with respect to dependency is quite different depending on which of the two Interpretation Functions proposed in 5.1.5 is chosen. We will begin by discussing the case of the first, $IF_{CG \rightarrow 1D}$, which identifies dependency and functor-argument structure, and then turn to the second, $IF_{CG \rightarrow 2D}$, which provides a separate notion of dependency.

Simple CGs are strongly equivalent to DG and SMCFGS with respect to dependency, under $IF_{CG \rightarrow 1D}$. We show this by proving (16) and (17).

(16) For every simple CG G there is a strongly equivalent MCFG G' with respect to dependency such that there is a finite bound on the length of head-paths in $\Sigma(G')$.

(17) For every DG G', there is a strongly equivalent CG G with respect to dependency.

PROOF OF (16)

We prove (16) by construction, using a construction similar to that given above for the proof of (12a). Let W be the subset of the set of categories defined by G that contains all of the categories assigned by A to elements of V_T in G, and all of the basic and intermediate categories required to construct these categories by the rules D. We take W as the nonterminal vocabulary of G'. We define P of G' as in (18).

(18) a. $\forall\ (X_1 \ldots X_{i\text{-}1} \setminus X_i \,/\, X_{i+1} \ldots X_n) \in W$,
$X_i \rightarrow X_1 \ldots X_{i\text{-}1}\ (X_1 \ldots X_{i\text{-}1} \setminus X_i \,/\, X_{i+1} \ldots X_n)'\ X_{i+1} \ldots X_n \in P$;
and
$X_i' \rightarrow X_1 \ldots X_{i\text{-}1}\ (X_1 \ldots X_{i\text{-}1} \setminus X_i \,/\, X_{i+1} \ldots X_n)'\ X_{i+1} \ldots X_n \in P$.

b. $\forall a \in V_T$, if a is assigned to category X by A in G, then $X \rightarrow a$ and $X' \rightarrow a \in P$.

It is obvious that there is a bijective mapping between the derivation sets of G and G' which preserves dependency. Indeed, the marked daughter in P always corresponds to the functor constituent in G. It is also obvious that the resulting MCFG satisfies the relevant condition on finite bounds. ■

PROOF OF (17)

We prove theorem (17) by construction. For every rule of type $B(A_1, ..., A_n * C_1, ..., C_m)$ in G', assign all lexical items assigned to category B by L in G' to the category $(A_1, ..., A_n \backslash B / C_1, ..., C_m)$ by A in G. For every rule of type $B(*)$ in G', assign all lexical items assigned to category B by L in G' to the category B by A in G. Obviously, this construction will produce a CG G which generates the same strings as G', assigning them the same dependency interpretations, under $IF_{CG \to 1D}$. ■

Let us now turn to the second, more natural definition of dependency provided by $IF_{CG \to 2D}$. The results here are more complex. Theorem (17) remains true, though the construction in the proof must be modified. The problem is that under the above construction, rules of the form $B(*B)$ and $B(B*)$ in a DG will lead to assigning terminals b_i of category B in the DG to the categories B/B and $B \backslash B$ respectively. But, in this case, this leads to the wrong assignment of dependency relations in the CG, given the original DG. To remedy this problem, it is sufficient to add an exception clause in the construction of the type: except if the dependency rule is of the form $B(*B)$ or $B(B*)$, in which case, all lexical items assigned to category B by L in G' must be assigned to the categories $(B \backslash B)$ and (B/B) respectively by A in G.

Theorem (16), on the other hand, no longer holds. This is because the new definition of head leads to a situation where there is no longer a finite bound on head paths in CG derivations. This is shown in Figure 5.6.

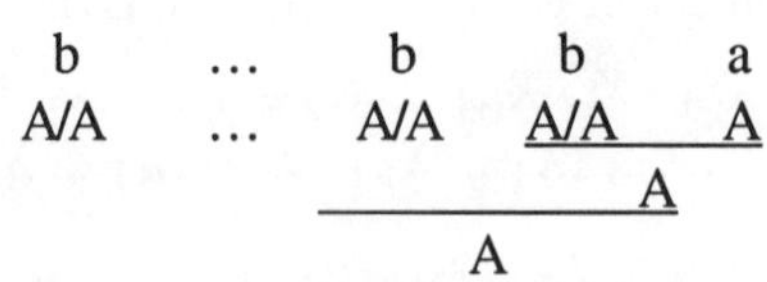

Figure 5.6

It is obvious from this figure that occurrence a is the head of the string $b^n a$ generated, and that there is no bound on the length of the head path from root to head lexical occurrence. Note also that as a corollary, there is no finite bound on the number of occurrences which can depend on another, all the b occurrences in Figure 5.6 depending on a. Consequently, the theorem (19) holds:

(19) DGs and SMCFGs are strongly included in CGs with respect to dependency, under $IF_{CG\rightarrow 2D}$.

At present, we have no results comparing CGs under $IF_{CG\rightarrow 2D}$ with MCFGs or XGBs, with respect to dependency and/or pairs of dependency and constituency interpretations.

5.2.3 Endocentricity

We have already remarked in section 5.1.3 above on the main difference between CGs and CFGs with respect to expressing adjunction structures. Namely, given the Interpretation Function $IF_{CG\rightarrow A}$ proposed for adjunction, all pairs $\langle\{E\}, E'\rangle$ in adjunct structures expressed by CGs will have a singleton as their first member. Moreover, the adjunct structures expressible by CGs are further indirectly restricted due to the restrictions on constituency imposed by CGs, with respect to CFGs. Consider for instance the CFG G with productions $S \rightarrow SS$, $S \rightarrow S\ B$, $S \rightarrow a$, $B \rightarrow b$. This grammar is a variant on the one discussed above with respect to the proof of (12a), generating the same set of derivations as the latter except that the structure $[_B\ b]$ can be adjoined to the right of any S node in the derivation. Obviously, because of the implicit relation between endocentricity and constituency, which imposes that if a set of occurrences is adjoined to another, both sets are constituents, no CG will be able to generate the same language as G while assigning the same adjunct structures to the strings. We can thus state the following theorem:

(20) CGs are strictly strongly included in CFGs with respect to endocentricity.

There remain many interesting results to be obtained in the comparison of simple CGs, XBGs and MCFGs with respect to to tuples of constituency, dependency and endocentricity interpretations, which we must leave for future research.

Chapter 6

Linking Systems

6.1 Introduction

In this chapter, I introduce a new Interpretation Domain ID_L for the analysis of what I will call *linking systems.*[1] In general terms, a linking system defined by a structural description is a relation on the constituent structure which it expresses. For example, the structural description in Figure 6.1, which is couched in a GPSG type formalism, expresses a linking system, specifically a filler-gap relation, which relates the constituent *that man* and the constituent ε. We note this linking system as the relation {⟨*that man*, ε⟩}, and we call the pair ⟨*that man*, ε⟩ a *link.*

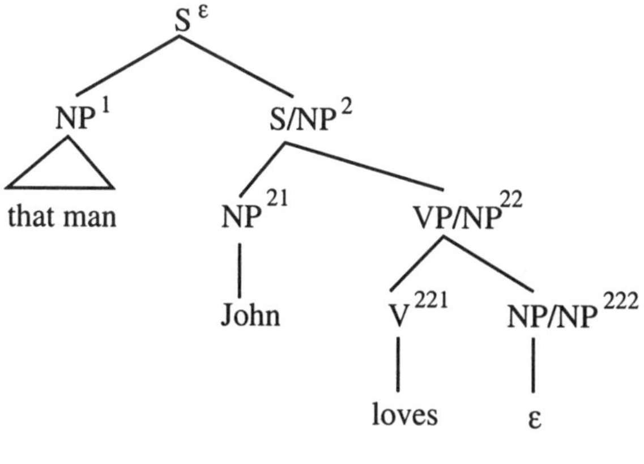

Figure 6.1

[1] The use of the term *link* here has its source in Peters and Ritchie 1982 and Joshi 1985. The latter discusses TAGs with links. It has not been possible for me to compare Joshi's results for TAGs with those presented here for other frameworks, though such a comparison would certainly produce very interesting results.

Figure 6.2 similarly defines a filler-gap relation, in this case, between the constituent *that man* and the pair of constituents ε_1 and ε_2. We can note this linking system as the relation $\{\langle$*that man*, $\{\varepsilon_1, \varepsilon_2\}\rangle\}$.

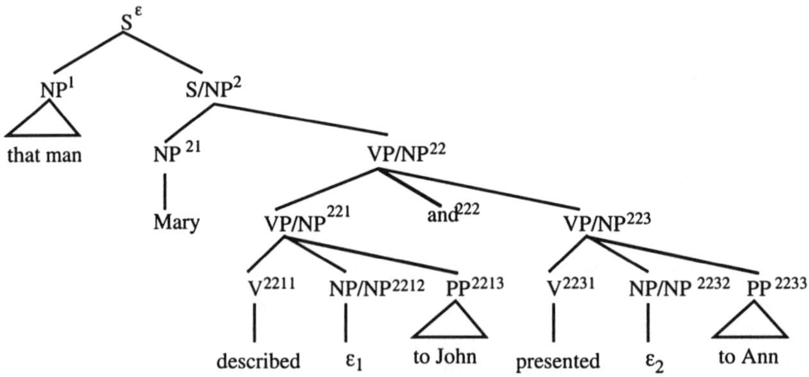

Figure 6.2

Figure 6.3 gives the structure of the Basque sentence given in (1).[2]

(1) Ikasle-ek harri-a bota z-u-te-n
student-pl.Erg stone-sg.Abs throw 3.Abs-aux-3.pl.Erg-past

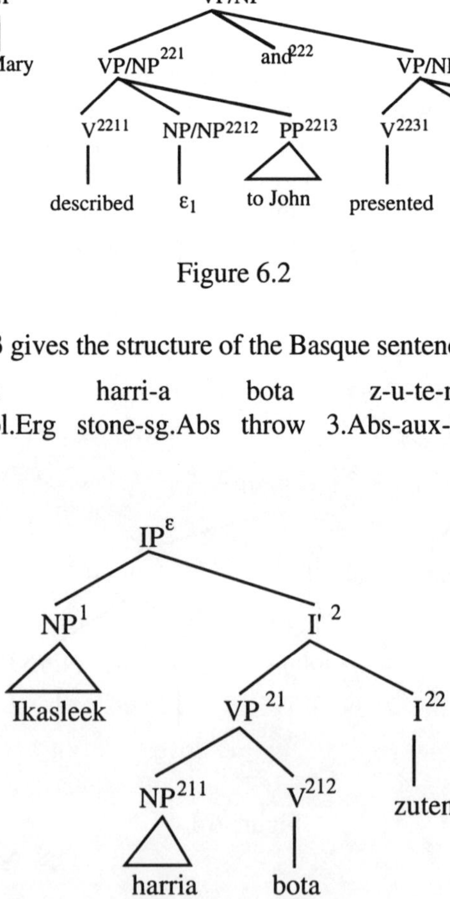

Figure 6.3

[2] Taken from Ortiz de Urbina (1989: 12, (20)).

The complete structural description for this sentence should express the agreement relation between the constituent *zuten* and its ergative and absolutive arguments *ikasleek* and *harria*. We can note this linking system as the relation {⟨*zuten*, ⟨*ikasleek*, *harria*⟩⟩} in which the first member is the agreement target, and the second member is the relevant tuple of agreement triggers.

More generally, let us define a linking system $\langle \mathfrak{L}, \Gamma \rangle$ as a *n*-placed relation $\mathfrak{L}$ over Γ, and/or the power set of Γ, $\wp(\Gamma)$, and/or the set of tuples of elements of Γ, Γ^n, where Γ is a constituent structure. When the constituent structure involved is obvious, we will simply note the linking system as $\mathfrak{L}$. We can then define the Interpretation Domain for linking systems ID_L as the set of all such pairs $\langle \mathfrak{L}, \Gamma \rangle$. This very general definition makes our definitions of dependency, endocentricity and function-argument structure special cases of linking systems. In this section, we will discuss the way linking systems can be used to characterize the SGC power of various formalism with respect to expressing filler-gap dependencies, and sketch how they can be used to characterize relations between agreement targets and agreement triggers, and antecedent-anaphor relations.[3]

6.1.1 Constituent Addresses and Node Addresses

Because linking systems are defined over constituent structures, it is useful to have a technique for characterizing relations between constituents in a general way, when discussing SGC with respect to linking. In order to do this, we will adopt a simple variant of the classical notion of *node addresses* for nodes in trees, due to Gorn.[4] Each node in a tree can be uniquely identified by a node address which is a string in N_0^*, that is the set of strings over the positive natural numbers N_0. The root node is identified by the empty string ε, and the address of the ith daughter of a node *n* is the result of concatenating the address of *n* with

[3] It is also possible to define what one could call *linear* linking systems, involving tuples of occurrence positions in strings, rather than constituents. This might be useful in discussing systems where there is no obvious constituent structure interpretation such as certain versions of Generalized Categorial Grammar. Note that any linking system of the type we are studying here directly defines a linear linking system, which is a much weaker notion.

[4] Cf. e.g. Gallier (1986: 13ff).

the number i to its right.[5] We adapt Gorn addressing to constituent structures as follows. Given a constituent structure Γ over a string of occurrences S, we assign the address ε to the constituent containing all of the occurrences in S. All other constituents, are assigned the address obtained by concatenating to the right of the address of the constituent in which they are immediately included the number representing their order in that constituent. We define the order of a constituent E_i immediately included in a constituent E as i if there are i-1 constituents $E_1 ... E_{i-1}$ immediately included in E such that all the occurrences in these constituents are to the left of all the occurrences in E_i.[6] Except in the case of trees with nonbranching local trees, this constituent addressing scheme gives the same results as Gorn addressing, and we will generally resort to the latter for perspicuity of representations, representing linking systems as relations involving tree addresses, rather than constituents. However, if there are nonbranching local trees, then, given the Interpretation Function for constituency adopted in section 2.5.2, more than one node will correspond to a given constituent, and consequently the Gorn addressing will not be the same as the constituent addressing proposed here.

6.1.2 Empty Constituents

In the illustrations of Figures 6.1 and 6.2, where the linking system characterizes a filler-gap dependency, the gap site is noted by ε. There are two classical ways of interpreting this notation. Either we consider ε to represent a phonetically empty but syntactically present formative, in which case nothing further needs to be said. Or, we assume that ε is to be interpreted as the empty string, i.e. that the position below the node NP/NP is simply not filled (e.g. that it is the result of the application of a

---

[5] When explicit notation of concatenation is useful, we use the symbol '.' as the concatenation operator. However, in most cases we can simply use juxtaposition. In particular, node addresses in trees can be unambiguously noted in base 10 using juxtaposition as long as nodes have 9 daughters or less.

[6] Note that this addressing scheme presupposes that the whole set of occurrences in S forms a constituent (cf. condition (2.4a) in section 2.5.1). It is obviously possible to extend the addressing system in order to obviate this requirement (using for instance the addressing scheme for multicomponent TAGs, cf. e.g. Weir 1988). It also crucially presupposes that conditions (2.4b) and (2.9), of section 2.7, barring overlapping constituents and discontinuous constituency, are met. The present addressing scheme is useless in discussing linking over constituent structures that do not meet the latter conditions.

null-productions $A \to \varepsilon$). If this is the desired interpretation, it is necessary to extend our definition of constituent structure to allow for such empty constituents. This can be done by allowing occurrences of the empty string ε (i.e. pairs of the form ⟨ε, *i*⟩) in the string of occurrences over which the constituent structure is defined. With this adjustment, the constituent structure corresponding to the tree in Figure 6.1 is that given in (2).

(2) {{⟨that, 1⟩, ⟨man, 2⟩, ⟨John, 3⟩, ⟨loves, 4⟩, ⟨ε, 5⟩}, {⟨that, 1⟩, ⟨man, 2⟩}, {⟨John, 3⟩, ⟨loves, 4⟩, ⟨ε, 5⟩}, {⟨loves, 4⟩, ⟨ε, 5⟩}, {⟨that, 1⟩}, {⟨man, 2⟩}, {⟨John, 3⟩}, {⟨loves, 4⟩}, {⟨ε, 5⟩}}

The presence of the empty occurrence ⟨ε, 5⟩ as a constituent in (2) makes the linking system {⟨*that man*, ε⟩}, expressed in Figure 6.1, a well-formed relation over constituents, and we can note it using the pair of constituent addresses ⟨1, 222⟩. Similarly, we note the linking systems expressed in Figures 6.2 and 6.3 as {⟨1, {2212, 2232}⟩} and {⟨22, ⟨1, 211⟩⟩} respectively. As will appear below, the use of constituent addresses in noting linking systems crucially simplifies the statement of constraints on links expressible by a given formalism, though it obviously lacks perspicuity in discussions of specific tree examples.

6.1.3 Constraints Between Linking and Constituency

Obviously, in a linking system $\langle \mathfrak{L}, \Gamma \rangle$, the choice of the relation $\mathfrak{L}$ and the constituent structure Γ are not independent. Specifically, it is obvious that if constituent addresses a_i, $1 \leq i \leq n$ appear in the statement of $\mathfrak{L}$, Γ must have the following properties:

(3) a. For all a_i, $1 \leq i \leq n$, and for every prefix p of a_i, Γ contains a constituent with address p.
   b. For all a_i, $1 \leq i \leq n$, if $a_i = q.j$, $j \in N_0$, then for all k, $k < j$, Γ contains a constituent with address $q.k$.

One consequence of this is that in most cases, simply stating the relation $\mathfrak{L}$ will be sufficient to provide much of the relevant information about the intended constituent structure Γ.

6.1.4 Command Constraints on Links

One classical type of constraint imposed by formalisms on links is usually discussed in terms of *command*. We can adopt the formal analysis of command relations proposed by Barker and Pullum 1990 as a framework for discussing such constraints. We need only make minor adjustments, restating their analysis in terms of relations over the constituents in constituent structures, rather than over nodes in trees. We will say that a linking system $\langle \mathfrak{L}, \Gamma \rangle$ obeys the command relation C_P over Γ if and only if for every link in $\mathfrak{L}$, all the fillers command all the gaps, more specifically:

(4) $\langle \mathfrak{L}, \Gamma \rangle$ obeys the command relation C_P over Γ iff $\forall \langle\langle f_1, ..., f_m \rangle, \langle g_1, ..., g_n \rangle\rangle \in \mathfrak{L}, \forall i, j, 1 \leq i \leq m, 1 \leq j \leq n, f_i\ C_P\ g_j$

For cases where all links are simply pairs of constituents (rather than pairs of tuples of constituents), $\mathfrak{L}$ satisfies the command relation C_P over Γ if and only if $\mathfrak{L}$ is included in C_P.

6.2 Linking Systems for Filler-Gap Dependencies

In a linking system $\langle \mathfrak{L}, \Gamma \rangle$, expressing filler-gap dependencies, Γ is a constituent structure and $\mathfrak{L} = \{\langle\langle f_1, ..., f_m \rangle, \langle g_1, ..., g_n \rangle\rangle, ...\}$ is a set of pairs of tuples of constituents, (in fact, technically, the f_i and g_j are constituent *addresses*, which are in bijective correspondence with the constituents). For every pair $\langle\langle f_1, ..., f_m \rangle, \langle g_1, ..., g_n \rangle\rangle$ in $\mathfrak{L}$, we interpret the f_i as the fillers and the g_j as gaps in a single filler-gap dependency. In the unmarked case, $m = n = 1$, as in Figure 6.1 above. But, we allow $n > 1$ in order to express cases where more than one gap corresponds to a filler (i.e. constructions such as 'Across-the-Board extraction' (ATB extraction) out of a coordinate structure, as in Figure 6.2, or parasitic gaps, as in (5a)). We allow $m > 1$ for cases where more than one filler corresponds to a gap (e.g. in the case of ATB extraction into a coordinate structure, as in (5b).[7] (5c) shows an example where both $m > 1$ and $n > 1$ and (5d) gives an example where there is more than one link.[8]

---

[7] The use of transformational terminology here is purely descriptive and is not intended to make any claims with respect to a choice of analysis.

[8] In these examples, I am not committing myself as to the exact nature of the constituent structures on which the links are defined.

(5) a. [Which reports] did you file ε_1 without reading ε_2?
$\mathfrak{L} = \{\langle\langle\{\text{which, reports}\}\rangle, \langle\{\varepsilon_1\},\{\varepsilon_2\}\rangle\rangle\}$

b. I wonder who$_1$ Mary thinks and who$_2$ Ann knows that John saw ε_1?
$\mathfrak{L} = \{\langle\langle\{\text{who}_1\},\{\text{who}_2\}\rangle, \langle\{\varepsilon_1\}\rangle\rangle\}$

c. I wonder who$_1$ Mary thinks and who$_2$ Ann knows that John saw ε_1 and Peter heard ε_2?
$\mathfrak{L} = \{\langle\langle\{\text{who}_1\},\{\text{who}_2\}\rangle, \langle\{\varepsilon_1\},\{\varepsilon_2\}\rangle\rangle\}$

d. I wonder [who$_1$ Mary saw ε_1] and [who$_2$ she did not see ε_2].
$\mathfrak{L} = \{\langle\langle\{\text{who}_1\}\rangle, \langle\{\varepsilon_1\}\rangle\rangle, \langle\langle\{\text{who}_2\}\rangle, \langle\{\varepsilon_2\}\rangle\rangle\}$

Given the intended interpretation of the gap constituents, in the second members of the pairs, it is clear that linking systems expressing filler-gap dependencies will impose constraint (6a) on the corresponding constituent structure, forbidding the presence of subconstituents of the gap constituent. Specifically, a gap constituent is always a singleton set, containing either an occurrence of a resumptive pronoun, or an occurrence of a phonetically empty morph, or an occurrence of the empty string (the choice between the latter two depending on the interpretation chosen for gaps, cf. section 6.1.2; in what follows, I will be making the former assumption, for concreteness, though nothing hinges on this). Furthermore, it is consistent with usual syntactic intuitions to forbid a constituent which is either a filler or a gap in a given link to be either a filler or a gap in another link, as expressed in (6b).

(6) If $\langle\mathfrak{L}, \Gamma\rangle$ is a linking system, then, if $\langle\langle f_1, \ldots, f_m\rangle, \langle g_1, \ldots, g_n\rangle\rangle \in \mathfrak{L}$,

a. there are no constituents in Γ with addresses of which g_i $1 \leq i \leq n$ is a prefix;

b. $\forall i, j$, $1 \leq i \leq m$, $1 \leq j \leq n$, there is no other pair in $\mathfrak{L}$ where f_i or g_j appears, either as a filler, or as a gap.

In what follows, for simplicity, we will limit our discussion to the case where $m = n = 1$. This allows us to define linking systems as sets pairs of constituents $\langle f, g\rangle$, where the first element is the filler and the second is the corresponding gap.

6.3 Linking Systems for Filler-Gap Dependencies in GPSG

In this section, we analyze what kinds of linking systems for filler gap dependencies can be defined by classical GPSG, as defined in GKPS. These authors constrain possible categories so that there can be only one SLASH feature (/) defined for each category label, and this feature can only take a single category as its value (as opposed to a list, a stack, or a set of categories, see discussion below). For our present purposes, we can ignore the internal structure of categories beyond the feature SLASH. We consider the set of categories K to be feature structures over two features CAT and /, both of which take atomic symbols from V_N as their value. All categories have the CAT feature in their domain, whereas the SLASH feature is optional. We note a category [CAT: A] simply as A, and a category [CAT: A, SLASH: B] as A/B. The Interpretation Function $IF_{GPSG \rightarrow L}$ will be defined so that a structural description σ defines a link $\langle p, q \rangle$ if and only if:

(7) a. There is an empty position in σ directly dominated by a node of the type A/A, with address q;
b. the latter node is the foot of a path consisting of nodes which all bear the feature $/A$; and
c. the node at the top of this path has a sister of category A with address p.

This situation is illustrated in Figure 6.1 above where A is NP, the foot of the path is the node NP/NP with address 222, the top of the path is node S/NP with address 2, and the NP with address 1 is the sibling of category A. The link defined is $\langle 1, 222 \rangle$.

In order to carry out subsequent proofs, let us precisely define the admissible types of rules. We will consider a version of GPSG that is simplified but that does not betray the original as far as the problems we are studying are concerned.[9]

A) Structural rules. Their general form is $A \rightarrow B_1 \ldots B_n$, where A, $B_1, \ldots, B_n \in K$. In particular, the following types are allowed:

(8) (i) $/ \notin \mathrm{Dom}(A)$; and (ii) $\neg \exists B_i\ 1 \leq i \leq n \mid / \in \mathrm{Dom}(B_i)$
(9) (i) $/ \in \mathrm{Dom}(A)$; and (ii) $A(/) = C$; and (iii) $C \neq A$; and
(iv) $\exists! B_i \mid / \in \mathrm{Dom}(B_i)$; and (v) $B_i(/) = C$
(10) (i) $/ \notin \mathrm{Dom}(A)$; and (ii) $\exists! B_i\ 1 \leq i \leq n \mid / \in \mathrm{Dom}(B_i)$; and
(iii) $B_i(/) = C$; and (iv) $\exists! B_j,\ i \neq j \mid B_j = C$

B) Lexical rules. Their general form is $A \rightarrow a$, with $A \in K$, $a \in V_T$. In particular, the following types are allowed:

(11) (i) $/ \notin \mathrm{Dom}(A)$; and (ii) $a \in V_T / \{\varepsilon\}$
(12) (i) $/ \in \mathrm{Dom}(A)$; and (ii) $A(/) = A$; and (iii) $a = \varepsilon$.

---

9 Except that, as mentioned above, we are ignoring the possibilities of linking systems involving more than one filler or more than one gap, as in parasitic gaps or ATB extraction cases.

The interpretation function $IF_{GPSG \to L}$ has as its domain the set of possible derivations in this restricted version of GPSG, and as its range, the Interpretation Domain for linking systems ID_L. It can be defined informally as follows: A local tree licensed by a rule of type (10) defines the top of a link. The node B_j is the filler and B_i is the first node in the path that goes down to the corresponding gap. The application of a rule of type (9) transmits information expressed by the feature SLASH on the presence of a gap. The application of a rule of type (12) defines the foot of a link, i.e. a category dominating a gap which corresponds to a filler. The other types of rules do not contribute to defining the linking system in the tree. Note the following points:

- Constraint (9iii) imposes the *A*-over-*A* constraint on extraction.
- Constraint (10ii) forbids cases where one antecedent corresponds to different empty positions (cf. fn. 9).
- Clause (10iv) could be modified so that rules with zero or one occurrence of *C* on the right hand side are admitted. This would be necessary in order to allow for the treatment proposed in GKPS for *tough*-movement constructions, such as 'John is easy to please ε'. However, in such cases, it is not clear a priori whether one would want to establish a link between 'John' and ε. The possible means of adapting the Interpretation Function in order to obtain such a result will not be examined here. I will consider that the top of a link is established by a rule satisfying (10i, ii, iii) only if it also satisfies (10iv).
- In order to obtain links with resumptive pronouns, rather than gaps, condition (iii) of (12) must be modified so as to allow resumptive pronouns below categories of the form *A*/*A*, in which case the category in question would be interpreted as the foot of the link. These pronouns must be excluded from appearing on the right hand side in rules of type (11).

The following theorem can be proved as to the linking systems definable in standard GPSGs; specifically, this theorem.defines the subset of ID_L which is the image of Σ(GPSG) by $IF_{GPSG \to L}$.[10]

---

[10] Notational conventions: $m, n, p, q, r \in N_0^*$, and $i, j, k \in N_0$ and $i \neq j$, $n^{\leq}$ is a prefix of n, and $n^{<}$ is a strict prefix of n.

THEOREM

(13) A linking system $\langle \mathfrak{L}, \Gamma \rangle$ can be defined by a structural description in a GPSG iff Γ can be produced by a CFG and $\mathfrak{L}$ satisfies the following conditions:

a. For all links $\langle p, q \rangle \in \mathfrak{L}$, $p = m.i$ and $q = m.j.n$.
b. If $\langle m.i, m.j.n \rangle \in \mathfrak{L}$, then none of the constituents $m.j.n^{<}.k$ may appear as first or second member of another link belonging to $\mathfrak{L}$.
c. The constituent m may not appear as second member in another link belonging to $\mathfrak{L}$.
d. If $\langle m.i, m.j.n \rangle \in \mathfrak{L}$, then no link in $\mathfrak{L}$ may have the form $\langle m^{\leq}.k, m.j.n^{<}.r \rangle$.

Condition (13a) enforces IDC-command (cf. Barker and Pullum 1990: 15) of the gap by the filler, in the constituent structure.[11] Condition (13b) forbids any constituent on the SLASH path from being a filler or a gap in another link, as well as any immediate constituent of a constituent on the SLASH path. Condition (13c) forbids the constituent directly dominating the filler from being a gap in another link. Finally, condition (13d) forbids the presence of links whose SLASH path would share constituents with that of another link. These properties can be illustrated on Figure 6.4, which illustrates a link between filler $C^{m.i}$ and gap $C/C^{m.j.n}$. Note that the former IDC-commands the latter. The SLASH path of this link is the path of nodes from $B_i/C^{m.j}$ to $C/C^{m.j.n}$.

The crucial point in this theorem is condition (13d), which prevents any overlapping of the paths between an antecedent and the empty node corresponding to it. Such situations would of course require categories with more than one SLASH feature (or SLASH features taking as values more than one category, cf. section 6.7), which is impossible in standard GPSG.

---

[11] Note that in this particular case IDC-command on the constituent structure corresponds to IDC-command on the corresponding tree structure. This is because the rules (10), defining the top of a link, are necessarily branching. In the general case, IDC-command on the constituent structure corresponds to C-command (cf. Barker and Pullum 1990: 14) on the corresponding tree, since in nonbranching local trees, the mother and daughter correspond to the same constituent.

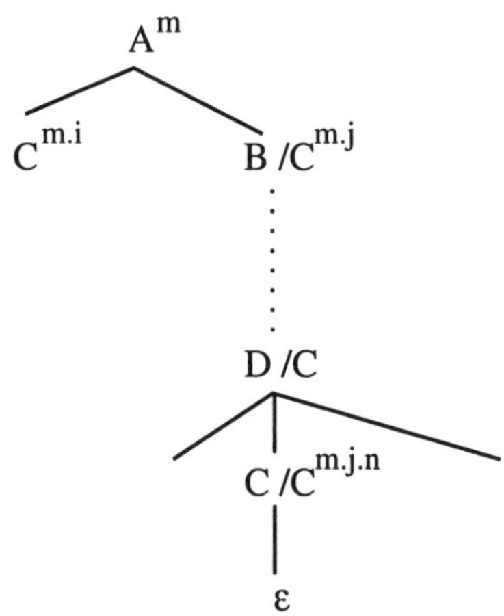

Figure 6.4

PROOF OF THEOREM (13)

Part I. Let us begin by proving the *only if* part of theorem (13) by induction on the construction of the linking system for a derivation.

First, the fact that the top of a link is necessarily associated with a local tree licensed by a rule of type (10) ensures the validity of the IDC-command constraint (13a).

Second, we prove that if there is a link ⟨*m.i*, *m.j.n*⟩, then there can be no links of types forbidden by (13b). The forbidden gap positions will be examined first, followed by the forbidden filler positions .

A. In order to dominate a new gap, a node must have the feature SLASH in its domain and the value of that feature must be the same as the CAT value of the node. Given the hypothesis that there is already a link of type ⟨*m.i*, *m.j.n*⟩ this will be impossible for the following positions:

a) All constituents of the type $m.j.n^{<}$, i.e. those on the SLASH path. Indeed these constituents have SLASH in the domain of their labels, but the value of SLASH cannot be identical to that of their label, because of constraint (9iii) (the '*A*-over-*A*' constraint).

b) All constituents of the type $m.j.n^{<}.k$ as well as the nodes *m.k*. Indeed, these constituents are obtained by rules of the types (9) and (10), which require that there be one and only one element with the feature

SLASH on the right hand side. But these constituents have a sibling with the feature SLASH in their domains by hypothesis.

c) The constituent *m.j.n*. By hypothesis, this node dominates the gap position of a first link, and by (6b), it cannot appear in a second link.

B. In order to dominate a new filler position, a node must be the result of the application of a rule of type (10). By hypothesis, this is not the case for any of the nodes mentioned in condition (13b).

Third, for the constituent *m*, (13c) is obvious: since a rule of type (10) applies to this node, SLASH cannot be in its domain (10i), and consequently, it cannot immediately dominate a gap.

Finally, fourth, in order for a link of the type forbidden by (13d) to be established, it would be necessary for the label of the constituent with address *m* to transmit the SLASH feature associated with that link, i.e. it would be necessary for that constituent to be the mother in a local tree licensed by a rule of type (9). This is impossible by hypothesis. ■

Part II. We now sketch a proof for the *if* part of theorem (13), i.e. we show that for any linking system $\langle \mathfrak{L}, \Gamma \rangle$ satisfying conditions (13a-d) there is a GPSG of the class defined above which generates a derivation defining that linking system. In section 6.1.3 above, a compatibility condition between $\mathfrak{L}$ and Γ was given. Furthermore, by hypothesis, Γ is such that it can be defined by a derivation in a CFG G. In order for the proof to go through, we simply need to show that we can add rules to G involving categories with SLASH in their domain so that the desired linking system can be expressed, as well as the constituent structure. The proof is by induction on the number of links in $\mathfrak{L}$.

A. Induction hypothesis.

If there is a single link in $\mathfrak{L}$, it is obvious that the rule set of the GPSG can be modified so that there is a path of SLASH labeled constituents between the filler and gap of that link.

B. Induction step.

If we have a GPSG G_i, generating a structural description that defines a linking system with set of i links $\mathfrak{L}_i$, then, given a set of links $\mathfrak{L}_{i+1}$, obtained from $\mathfrak{L}_i$ by adding a new link $\langle p, q \rangle$ it is clear that we can modify the rule set of G_i, in order to obtain G_{i+1}, which generates a structural description that defines $\mathfrak{L}_{i+1}$. This is possible because conditions (13b,c,d) are such that they ensure that it is never necessary to add more than one occurrence of SLASH to the label of a constituent. ■

6.4 Linking Systems for Filler-Gap Dependencies in Parenthesis-free Categorial Grammars.

In many versions of Generalized Categorial Grammar, discussing linking systems based on constituency is not an obviously feasible enterprise because of the multiple constituent structures available for a single sentence. However, the class of CGs studied with respect to WGC by Friedman et al. 1986, which they call parenthesis-free, do not present this problem since their reduction rules are such that there is a unique structure for each assignment of lexical categories to a sentence. These grammars were introduced in Ades and Steedman 1982. They use only one connective, right division '/'. Complex categories do not have any parentheses: a category such as $A/B/C$ is always implicitly interpreted as meaning $((A/B)/C)$. A category of type $(A/(B/C))$ is thus impossible.

Formally, a parenthesis-free CG is a 6-tuple $\langle BC, D, R, V_T, A, S\rangle$, as in chapter 5. The set *CD* of derivable categories for a grammar *G* is defined as the set of all the categories that may appear in derivations in *G*.

The reduction rules R are the following:[12]

(14) a. $U/A \;\; A \Rightarrow U$ (rule **F**)
b. $U/A \;\; A/B \Rightarrow U/B$ (rule $\mathbf{FP_2}$)
c. $A \;\; U/A \Rightarrow U$ (rule **B**)

Ades and Steedman 1982 use a restricted version of **B**, **Bs**, in which either $U = S$ or $U = S/V$. I will investigate the more general case, however. Note also that in a later paper (Steedman 1985), Steedman uses a more general version of $\mathbf{FP_2}$, called **FP** by Friedman et al.

(15) $U/A \;\; A/V \Rightarrow U/V$ (rule **FP**)

Friedman et al. 1986 prove that grammars with **F**, $\mathbf{FP_2}$ and **B** generate only a subset of the CFLs, but that grammars allowing the more general rule **FP** can generate non-context-free languages. Such grammars also allow very powerful linking systems (cf. Steedman 1985 on crossing dependencies in Dutch), and I will not discuss them further in this study.

Figures 6.5, 6.6 and 6.7 below illustrate typical derivations in a parenthesis-free Categorial Grammar.

---

[12] Notational conventions are the following: *U*, *V* denote atomic or complex categories; *A*, *B*, *C* denote atomic categories.

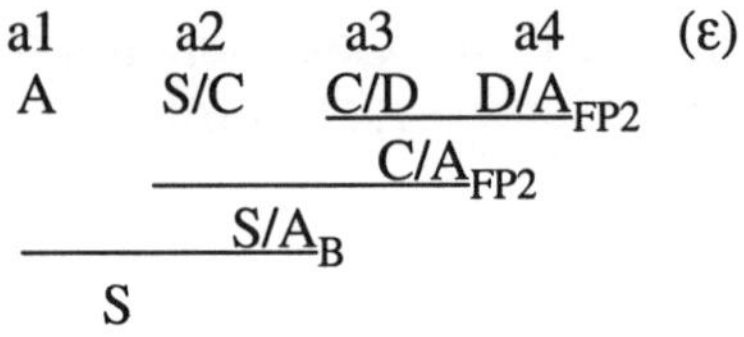

Figure 6.5

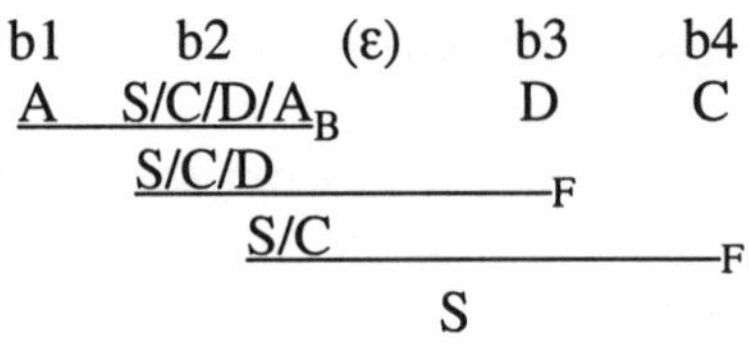

Figure 6.6

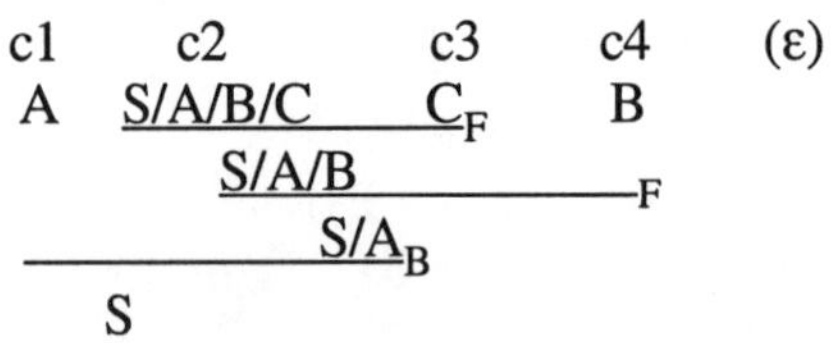

Figure 6.7

In accordance with the intentions of Ades and Steedman 1982, when rule **B** is applied, the argument category will be interpreted as a filler which is the antecedent of an empty position. The empty position in question has been indicated by an ε in the derivations in Figures 6.5, 6.6, and 6.7. The fillers are respectively a_1, b_1 and c_1. More generally, I will consider that the empty position corresponding to a filler constituent *A* is situated in the position *T* such that if *A* had been in *T*, the sentence could have been accepted without using rule *B*.

Given these properties, I define linking systems in parenthesis-free categorial grammars on the basis of constituent structures defined by the following Interpretation Function, which provides empty occurrences in the strings as illustrated in the above derivations and integrates them into the constituent structure, as illustrated in Figure 6.8, 6.9 and 6.10 below. I will interpret derivations in parenthesis-free CGs for constituency as in section 5.1.2, except that if there is an element *a* of category $U = V/A$

followed by an empty position ε, *a* will be interpreted as a constituent of category *U* and ε as a constituent of category *A*, and the string *a*ε as a constituent of category *U*. This definition presupposes that one can independently establish whether there are empty positions in the terminal string. In a parenthesis-free CG, this is completely unproblematic. I will consider that there is an empty position behind any substring that reduces to a category of type *V/A* which is in turn reduced by a rule **B**. It is easy to check that this gives the desired results for the derivations given in Figures 6.5, 6.6, and 6.7.

With these preliminaries, we can state the following theorem.

THEOREM

(16) Parenthesis-free CGs, with rules **F**, $\mathbf{FP_2}$ and **B**, are strictly included in SGC in GPSGs with respect to linking systems and constituent structure.

A detailed proof by construction of this theorem can be found in Miller (1990: 225ff). Here, I will just sketch the construction.

For every parenthesis-free CG $G = \langle BC, D, R, V_T, A, S\rangle$, with rules **F**, $\mathbf{FP_2}$ and **B**, there is a GPSG $G' = \langle V_N, V_T, F, S, R\rangle$ which is strongly equivalent to G with respect to linking systems and constituent structure.[13]

Let $V_N = CD \cup \{U[/A] \mid U \in CD \text{ and } A \in BC\}$. We take F to be the set of features {CAT, SLASH}, where both features take their values in V_N The set R of productions is defined as follows:

(17) a. $\forall a \in V$, if $U \in A(a)$, then $U \rightarrow a \in R$
b. $\forall U/A \in CD,\ U \rightarrow U/A\ \ A \in R$
c. $\forall U/A \in CD,\ U/A \rightarrow U/B\ \ B/A \in R$
d. $\forall U/A \in CD,\ U \rightarrow A\ \ U/A[/A] \in R$
e. $\forall U/A \in CD,\ U/A[/A] \rightarrow U/B\ \ B/A[/A] \in R$
f. $\forall U/A \in CD,\ U/A[/A] \rightarrow U/A\ \ A[/A] \in R$
g. $\forall A \in BC,\ A[/A] \rightarrow \varepsilon \in R$

We can informally define the relationship between derivations in both grammars as follows. Rules of type (17a) correspond to the lexical assignment function *A*. Those of types (17b,c) simulate **F** and $\mathbf{FP_2}$. Rules of type (17d) replace **B**, introducing a SLASH feature which

---

[13] In order to distinguish the categorial connective '/' from the slash feature, I will note a GPSG category with value *B* for the feature slash and value *A* for the feature CAT as *A*[/*B*].

makes it possible to preserve the information on the corresponding empty position. Rules of type (17e) simulate **FP2**, transmitting a SLASH feature. Those of type (17f) terminate the path of a SLASH feature and create a node that dominates an empty position. This construction is illustrated in Figures 6.8, 6.9 and 6.10 below which exhibit the GPSG derivations corresponding to the derivations in Figures 6.5, 6.6 and 6.7 respectively.

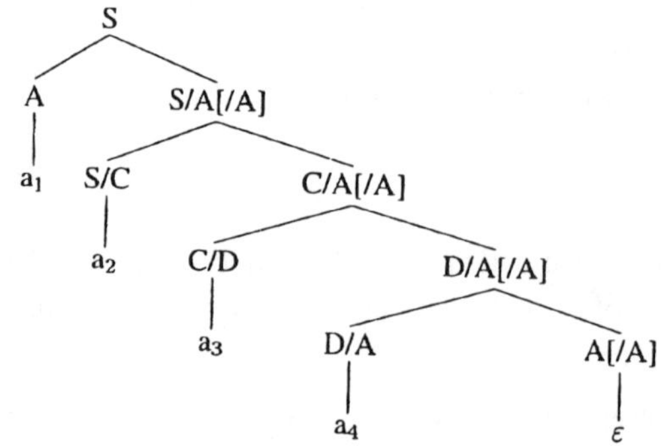

Figure 6.8

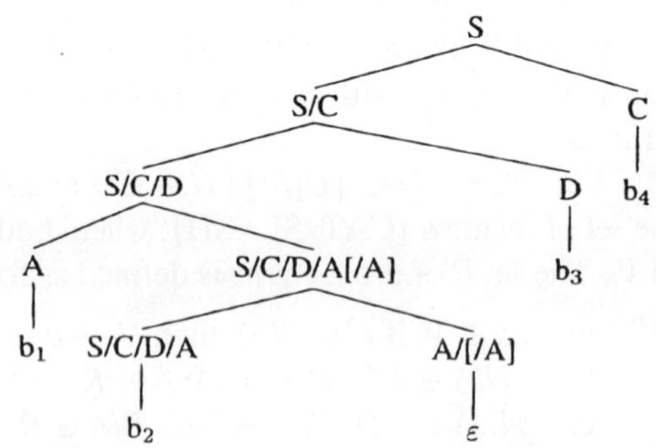

Figure 6.9

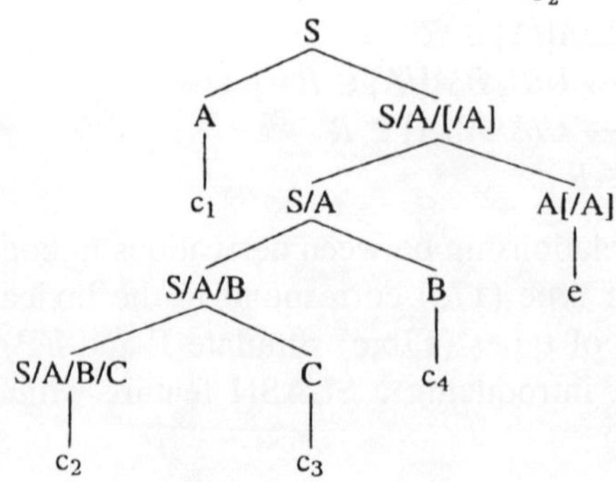

Figure 6.10

6.5 Linking Systems for Filler-Gap Dependencies in Transformational Grammars

In this section I will briefly discuss how linking systems for filler-gap dependencies can be defined for transformational grammars (TGs), and suggest rather informally the nature of some of the constraints bearing on them.

A structural description in a TG is a tuple of structures comprising the D-structure, the S-structure, the LF-structure the PF-structure, and perhaps various intermediate structures. Note that not all of these levels may be considered to be relevant parts of the structural description, in that all of the information they contain may be legitimately derivable from another level. This may be the case for e.g. D-structure. Structural descriptions in TGs thus define a tuple of constituent structures, corresponding to the different relevant levels of structure.

In TG with movement traces, linking systems can be defined by interpreting the S-structure (I am ignoring the possibility of LF movement here, but obviously the same kind of strategies as those which follow would be applicable to its analysis). By contrast with the systems that we have studied up to here, most versions of TG involve the notion of cyclic movement, i.e. the idea that movement from the original D-structure position to the S-structure position may be the result of a series of more local instances of movement. We can account for this idea by allowing links with a tuple of gaps per filler $\langle C_1, \langle C_2, ..., C_n\rangle\rangle$ and interpreting constituent C_n as the D-structure position of the filler C_1 and $C_{n\text{-}1}$ to C_2 as the various intermediate positions occupied by the filler in intermediate structures (thus, a pair $\langle C_1, \langle C_2, ..., C_n\rangle\rangle$ characterizes a 'chain' in transformational terminology). Obviously, interpretations involving cyclic movement are inherently richer than those discussed previously. Consequently, it is necessary to define a more structured Interpretation Domain $\mathrm{ID_{CL}}$ representing these types of structures. Note however, that there is a clearly defined (surjective) correspondence between $\mathrm{ID_{CL}}$ and $\mathrm{ID_L}$: any link of the form $\langle C_1, \langle C_2, ..., C_n\rangle\rangle$ will correspond to a link $\langle C_1, C_n\rangle$, and consequently, any linking system in $\mathrm{ID_{CL}}$ will correspond to a linking system in $\mathrm{ID_L}$. This means that there are legitimate interpretations of TG derivations into $\mathrm{ID_L}$, and that it is possible to relevantly compare the two classes of systems with respect to the linking interpretations they allow for ⟨'deep' filler, 'surface' gap⟩ pairs, using the transformational terminology.

Note that the notions just developed for cyclic movement must be generalized in the obvious ways to allow for fillers corresponding to multiple D-structure positions and/or intermediate positions, and for multiple fillers and/or intermediate positions corresponding to a single D-structure position (as in the cases of ATB extraction into or out of a coordinate structure).

Two types of questions arise: (i) What subsets of ID_{LC} and ID_L can be captured by various classes of TGs? (ii) How do various classes of TGs compare with other systems in these respects. In this section, I will simply make a series of preliminary remarks showing some of the types of restrictions that TGs impose on their linking systems, and give a general outline of how they can be reformulated within the present framework of analysis. Deeper results in this domain must await more extensive research. Obviously, working out the details of what these constraints actually mean depends on making explicit decisions on the various concepts involved, e.g. command, government (see Barker and Pullum 1990 for technical discussion of some possible choices in this respect, and Stabler 1992 for explicit decisions).

- In most versions of TG, movement can only take place from a position to another position that c-commands it. Consequently, for all links $\langle C_1, \langle C_2, ..., C_n\rangle\rangle$ defined by an S-structure S, all pairs $\langle C_i, C_{i+1}\rangle$ are such that there is a constituent K in $IF_{LC}(S)$, such that both C_i and C_{i+1} are included in K, and there is no constituent K' in $IF_{LC}(S)$, such that K includes K' and K' includes C_i. (Note this imposes classical c-command, other options are possible.)
- Movement is subject to subjacency. For all links $\langle C_1, \langle C_2, ..., C_n\rangle\rangle$ defined by an S-structure S, all pairs $\langle C_i, C_{i+1}\rangle$ are such that there are not two constituents K_1 and K_2 in $IF_{LC}(S)$ such that C_{i+1} is included in both K_1 and K_2, and C_i is included in neither K_1 and K_2, and the labels of K_1 and K_2 are both bounding labels.
- Traces must be properly governed. For all links $\langle C_1, \langle C_2, ..., C_n\rangle\rangle$ defined by an S-structure S, all pairs $\langle C_i, C_{i+1}\rangle$ are such that either (i) C_{i+1} is governed by a constituent which has a label belonging to the class of lexical governors (this is the case of 'lexical government'); or (ii) C_{i+1} is governed by C_i (this is the case of 'antecedent government'). The relevant notion of government can be defined in terms of constraints on constituency and labeling.
- Only one position in a chain is case-marked. This means that all links defined by an S-structure will be such that only one constituent among the C_i will be in the relevant structural configuration ('government') with respect to a case marking labeled constituent.

- Only one position in a chain is theta-marked. This constraint is similar to the preceding one, except that it involves a constituent whose labeling and position makes it a theta assigner, rather than a case assigner.
- Only zero-level and maximal projections can undergo movement, and they can only move to a position of identical bar level. This constraint can obviously be stated in terms of the labeling of the constituents in the links.

It should be noted that such constraints, in combination with constraints on well formed labeled constituent structures can lead to various kinds of constraints on possible co-existence of links within the linking system for a sentence, such as the 'doubly-filled COMP' constraint of Chomsky 1973, which in effect forces the same type of non-overlapping paths constraint on links as was discussed for classical GPSG grammars.

6.6 Linking Systems Without Gaps: LFG and HPSG-3

A variety of recent theories have proposed that filler-gap dependencies should be understood as involving no syntactic gap site in the constituent structure. The semantical and syntactic status of the filler with respect to the rest of the sentence is established by other means. This is the case e.g. in Lexical Functional Grammar LFG (cf. Bresnan 1982, Kaplan and Zaenen 1989) and in the latest version of HPSG (HPSG-3, cf. Pollard and Sag 1994, chapter 9). In both cases, however, the nature of the structural descriptions chosen makes it possible to study in an interesting way the kinds of relations that are allowed between a filler, and given position in the constituent structure, namely that constituent in the structural description which corresponds to the constituent which would directly dominate the empty constituent in a theory making use of gaps, namely the constituent to which the filler contributes its semantic value (this notion is made precise in different ways in HPSG and LFG, but the idea is obvious).

Consider for instance the structure in Figure 6.11 corresponding to Figure 6.1, but without the gap, which is essentially what is postulated in HPSG-3.

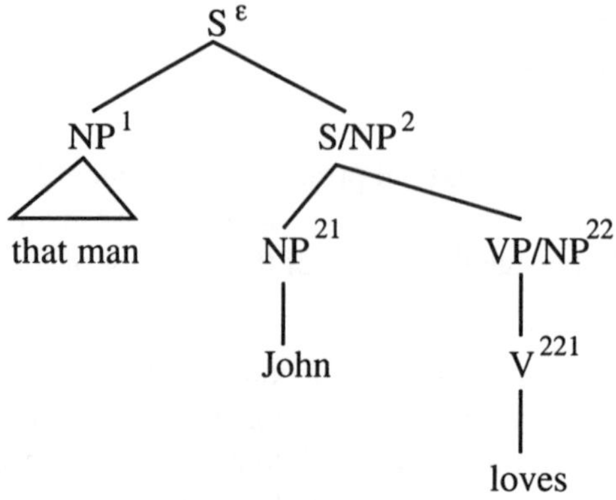

Figure 6.11

Given the intended interpretation of the SLASH feature, which is essentially identical to that in GKPS, it is obvious that this structure defines a link between the constituents NP^1 and VP/NP^{22}.

If one adopted constraints on possible paths of SLASH features in HPSG which were similar to those of GPSG, we would obviously be able to obtain a set of essentially parallel results on possible linking systems, expressing relations between the filler and the constituent to which it contributes its semantic value, rather than between the filler and a gap. However, Pollard and Sag 1994 postulate a set value for the SLASH feature, which leads to a much more powerful expression of linking. This will be briefly discussed in section 6.7.5 below.

Similarly, in LFG, the combination of the C-structure and the F-structure allow us to define linking systems similar to those just suggested for HPSG. Thus, the combination of the C-structure in Figure 6.12 and the F-structure in Figure 6.13 (both taken from Kaplan and Zaenen 1989: 29-30), obviously allows one to define a link between the NP constituent *Mary* and the VP constituent *telephoned*. The link is defined explicitly in the F-structure, and via the correspondence established between the two, it is also defined on the C-structure.

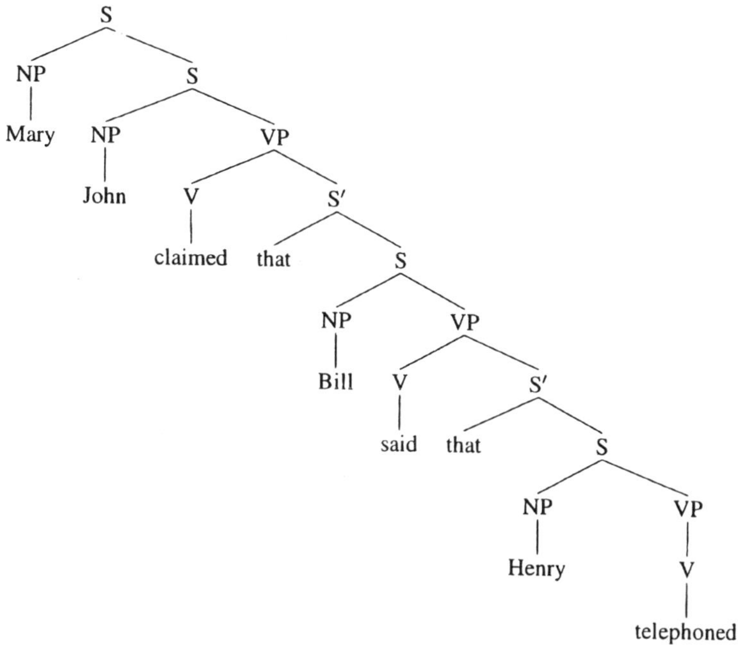

Figure 6.12

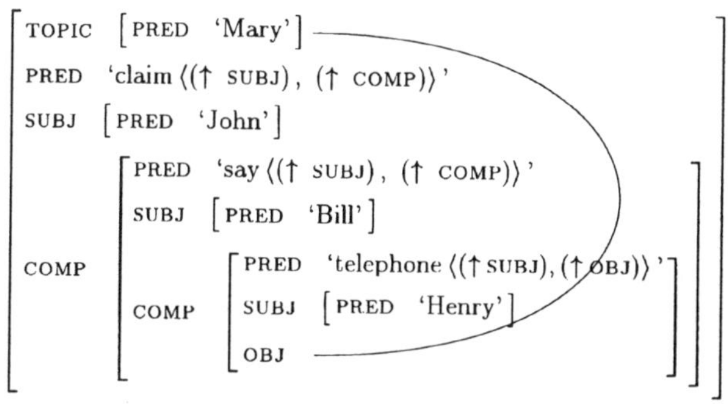

Figure 6.13

The constraints on possible links in LFG grammars are expressed by conditions on F-structures, stated in the form of equations (cf. Kaplan and Zaenen 1989) and, as was just noted, these equations establish corresponding constraints on possible links in the associated C-structures. Interesting research remains to be done in order to characterize the classes of linking systems definable by LFGs over

C-structures, and to compare them in the expressive power with other formalisms.

6.7 Linking systems for Filler-Gap Dependencies in EPSGs with Stacks of Slash Features

6.7.1 Introduction

Different studies (Maling and Zaenen 1982, Gazdar 1988, Miller 1991) have shown that categories carrying stacks of slash features are necessary in Extended Phrase Structure Grammars (EPSGs) in order to treat certain constructions in natural languages, while assigning them a reasonable constituent structure. One well known case is that of unbounded dependencies in Scandinavian languages. Maling and Zaenen exhibit Swedish and Norwegian sentences having linking systems of the type shown in Figure 6.14.

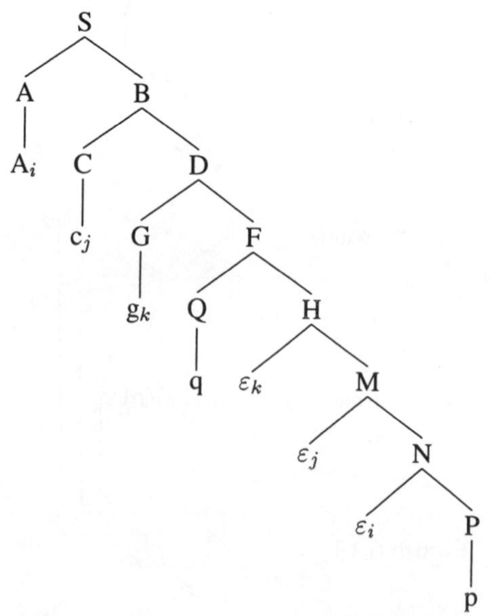

Figure 6.14

Furthermore, Maling and Zaenen give arguments suggesting that any number of links can be center-embedded as in Figure 6.14, as far as competence is concerned. It is clear that such structures violate conditions (13) on linking systems definable in standard GPSGs and that they consequently go beyond the capacity of standard GPSGs as far as SGC in terms of linking is concerned. However, it is possible to account for such structures if stacks of SLASH features, and rules that can add or remove such features from the stacks, are allowed. This will result in derivations such as the one exhibited in Figure 6.15.

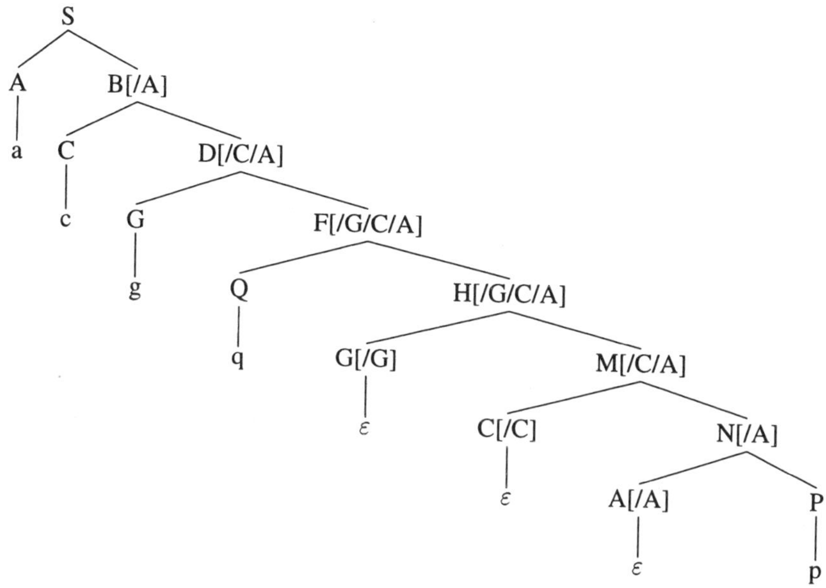

Figure 6.15

It is important to note though that such an extension of the GPSG formalism has substantial consequences from the point of view of weak generative capacity. It makes it possible for noncontext-free languages to be generated.

Gazdar 1988 has shown that the Indexed Grammars (IGs) of Aho 1968 allow an adequate formalization of EPSGs using stacks of SLASH features. IGs generate a set of languages (the ILs) that is a strict superset of the CFLs and a strict subset of the Context-Sensitive Languages (CSLs). Derivations in such grammars are similar to those in CFGs except that a stack of indices is associated to the elements of V_N. The indices belong to a set I which is disjoint from both V_N and V_T. Following Gazdar, we analyze the slash features (/*A*, /*B*,...) as indices.[14]

In the formulation given by Gazdar 1988 IGs allow the following types of productions:

(18) i. $A[\omega] \rightarrow W[\omega]$
ii. $A[\omega] \rightarrow V[\,]\, B[\omega]\, W[\,]$
iii. $A[\omega] \rightarrow V[\,]\, B[i\omega]\, W[\,]$
iv. $A[i\omega] \rightarrow W[\omega]$
v. $A[i\omega] \rightarrow V[\,]\, B[\omega]\, W[\,]$
vi. $A[\,] \rightarrow \mathrm{a}$

Rules of type (18.i) transmit the stack of indices on A to each of its daughters. Those of type (18.ii) transmit the stack on A to one of its daughters (B), and assign empty stacks to the others. Productions of type (18.iii) transmit the stack on A to one of its daughters, adding the index i to the stack in the process. Those of type (18.iv) transmit the stack on A, minus the index i that is on top of the stack, to all of its daughters (a production of this type may apply to an element A in V_N if, and only if, it has index i on the top of its stack). The rules of type (18.v) are similar to those of type (18.iv) except that the stack is transmitted to only one daughter. The lexical productions (18.vi) may only apply to elements of V_N if their stack is empty.

Three variants of IGs will now be examined, which differ from the standard definition in the types of productions and indices that are authorized. However, it is easy to show that their WGC is included in that of indexed grammars, since the new types of productions can be replaced by finite groups of rules of type (18) having the same effect. The productions considered in these formalisms are the following.

(19) $A[\omega] \rightarrow V[\,]\, B[\omega]\, W[\,]$

(20) $A[\omega] \rightarrow V[\,]\, B[/C\omega]\, W[\,]$, where either V contains one and only one occurrence of C and W contains no occurrence of C or W contains one and only one occurrence of C and V contains no occurrence of C.

---

[14] Notational conventions are the following: $a, b, c, ... \in V_T$; $A, B, C, ..., C_1, C_2 ... \in V_N$; ..., $V, W, X, Y, Z \in V_N{}^*$; $i, j, ... \in I$, $/A$, $/B$, ... $\in I$; ..., $\phi, \psi, \omega \in I^*$; the stack of indices associated with an element of V_N is placed behind it, between square brackets: $C[/A/B]$ is a category C with a stack $[/A/B]$; $[\,]$ represents the empty stack; if $W = ABC...$, $W[\omega]$ is an abbreviation for $A[\omega]\, B[\omega]\, C[\omega]...$

(21) a. $A[/C\omega] \to V[\,]\ C[/C]\ W[\,]\ B[\omega]\ X[\,]$
b. $A[/C\omega] \to V[\,]\ D[/C]\ W[\,]\ B[\omega]\ X[\,]$
c. $A[/C_1/C_2.../C_i\omega] \to V[\,]\ D[/C_1/C_2.../C_i]\ W[\,]\ B[\omega]\ X[\,],\ i \geq 1$

(22) a. $A[/C\omega] \to V[\,]\ B[\omega]\ W[\,]\ C[/C]\ X[\,]$
b. $A[/C\omega] \to V[\,]\ B[\omega]\ W[\,]\ D[/C]\ X[\,]$
c. $A[/C_1/C_2.../C_i\omega] \to V[\,]\ B[\omega]\ W[\,]\ D[/C_1/C_2.../C_i]\ X[\,],\ i \geq 1$

(23) $A[/A] \to \varepsilon$

(24) $A[\,] \to a$

As for the indices, they will all be of the form $/A$, $A \in V_N$. We thus have three classes of grammars, IGa, IGb and IGc, depending on whether variants (a), (b) or (c). of the rules (21) and (22) are chosen. Obviously, IGa is strictly included in IGb which is in turn strictly included in IGc.[15]

Let us define the Interpretation Function $IF_{IG \to L}$, which maps derivations in these grammars into ID_L in the following way: Application of a rule of type (20) creates the top of a link, the occurrence of C being the filler. Application of rules (19), (20), (21a,b,c), (22a,b,c) percolate the slash features in the tree, (for (19), (20), (21a) and (22a), the slash features transmitted are those represented by ω; for (21b) and (22b) the features transmitted are $/C$ and those in ω; for (21c) and (22c) the features transmitted are $/C_1/C_2.../C_i$ and those in ω. The application of rules (21a) and (22a) defines the foot of a link, by transmitting a single SLASH feature onto a node with the same label as the value of the feature; that node will dominate an empty position, by a rule of type (23). Let us now study the different types of linking systems that can be obtained when one chooses rules of type (a), (b) or (c). for (21) and (22).

---

[15] We thus eliminate production types (18.i) and (18.iv) which allow a stack to be transmitted to all of the daughters of a node. The resulting grammars are known as Linear Indexed Grammars (LIGs), and are known to be weakly equivalent to TAGs (cf. Vijayashanker 1987: 78ff.). The languages generated by LIGs are strictly included in the set of ILs. It would also have been possible to simply add the new types of productions considered to (18). This would have allowed us to keep as WGC the entire class of ILs. But, given the interpretation in terms of linking that is presented below for derivations using these new productions, such a strategy would have resulted in authorizing links where several empty positions correspond to one antecedent. This goes beyond the scope of the present study, though, as previously mentioned, there are potential applications to empirical phenomena.

6.7.2 Indexed Grammars of Type IGa

We prove the following theorem on the types of linking systems that can be characterized by IGs of the subclass IGa:[16]

THEOREM

(25) A linking system $\langle \mathfrak{L}, \Gamma \rangle$ can be defined by a structural description in a grammar of type IGa if, and only if, $\mathfrak{L}$ satisfies the following conditions:

a. If the link $\langle m.i, m.j.n \rangle \in \mathfrak{L}$, then none of the following nodes can appear in another link $\langle p, q \rangle$ as filler p:
(i) $m.k$; (ii) $m.j.n^{<}.k$; (iii) $m.j.n^{<}$.

b. If the link $\langle m.i, m.j.n \rangle \in \mathfrak{L}$, then none of the following nodes can appear in another link $\langle p, q \rangle$ as gap q:
(i) m ; (ii) $m.k$; (iii) $m.j.n^{<}$; (iv) $m.j.k$; (v) $m.j.n^{-1}.k$, with $k \neq \mathrm{h}$ where the daughter $B[\omega]$ in (21a) and (22a) is the hth element on the right hand side of these rules.

c. If the link $\langle m.i, m.j.n \rangle \in \mathfrak{L}$, then no link of the following types may appear in $\mathfrak{L}$:
 (i) $\langle m^{<}.k, m.j.n^{-1<}.r \rangle$;
 (ii) $\langle m.j.n^{<}.k, m.j.n^{<}.r \rangle$, with $|r| > 1$;
 (iii) if, moreover, there are links $\langle m^{<}.k, m.j.n^{-1}.r \rangle$ or $\langle m.j.n^{<}.k, m.j.n^{-1}.h \rangle$, then there may not be a link of type (c.i) with $q = m.j.n^{-1}.h$, nor a link of type (c.ii) with r of length 1.

The crucial point of this theorem is condition (25c), which can be informally described as forbidding the existence of pairs of links such that their paths between filler and gap overlap without one being included in the other.

PROOF OF THEOREM (25)

If $\mathfrak{L}$ contains the link $\langle m.i, m.j.n \rangle$, then a rule of type (20) was necessarily applied to the node with address m, rules of type (21a) or (22a) were applied to node $m.j.n^{-1}$, and rules of types (19), (20), (21a) or

---

16 Notational conventions: $m, n, p, q, r \in \mathrm{N}_0^*$, and $h, i, j, k \in \mathrm{N}_0$ and $i \neq j$, $n^{\leq}$ is a prefix of n, and $n^{<}$ is a strict prefix of n; n^{-1} is the sequence n with the last element removed.

(22a) to the nodes $m.j.n^{-1<}$ of the path between these two nodes. This situation is illustrated in Figure 6.16, which helps to follow the proof.

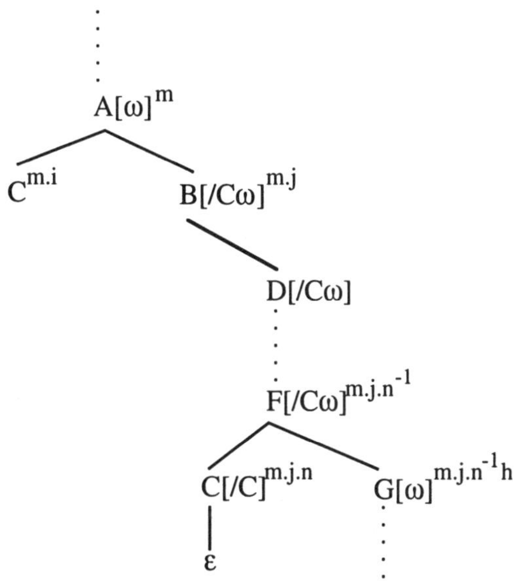

Figure 6.16

I. PROOF OF THE *ONLY IF* PART OF THEOREM (25):

(25a) and (25b) are trivial, given the structure of the rules authorized, and can easily be checked with reference to Figure 6.16. As for (25c), it is easy to see that in order to obtain the excluded links, forbidden manipulations of the index stack would be required: For a link of type (i), it would be necessary for a SLASH feature to have been put on the stack before the one defining the given link, and for the former to be taken off the stack before the latter. For a link of type (ii), with $n^{<} \neq n^{-1}$, it would be necessary for a slash feature to have been put on the stack after the one defining the given link, and for it to be taken off the stack after the latter. For a link of type (ii) with $n^{<} = n^{-1}$, one would have to ignore the restrictions on (21a) and (22a), that require that an index taken off the stack must be placed on a node with the same label as that index. The latter node must then be rewritten by a rule of type (23). To prove (iii), it is first necessary to notice that the feet of two separate links may be brothers, following an application of one of the rules (21a) or (22a), if, and only if, $\omega = /B$ in that rule. In that case, the stack contains just two indices before the application of the rule, and, when the one that is on the top of the stack is popped, the other is transmitted onto a node with the same label as itself. That node will then be rewritten by a rule of type (23). Such a situation is impossible, though, if there is a third link in the system of the type specified in (iii). In that case, there would be three links on the stack of the node to which the rule (21a) or (22a) is applied.■

II. PROOF OF THE *IF* PART OF THEOREM 4:

The proof for this part of the theorem is similar to that given in the *if* part of theorem (13), except that in this case, it is condition (25c) which ensures that the constraints on pushing and popping indexes on the stack are not violated, and that it is thus possible to create the necessary rules. ■

With these grammars, it is possible to obtain linking systems of the type exhibited in Figure 6.15. It is impossible, however, to obtain systems such as that shown in Figure 6.17 on the next page, for which Maling and Zaenen give examples (cf. Maling and Zaenen 1982: 242). The rule applied to node *G* in that figure ignores the constraints on rules (21a) and (22a). In order to account for such cases, grammars of type IGb are required.

6.7.3 Indexed Grammars of Type IGb

We prove the following theorem on the types of linking systems that can be characterized by IGs of the subclass IGa:

THEOREM

(26) A linking system $\langle \mathfrak{L}, \Gamma \rangle$ can be defined by a structural description in a grammar of type IGb if, and only if, $\mathfrak{L}$ satisfies (25a,b) and the following condition:
If the link $\langle m.j.n.f, m.j.n.g.r.s \rangle \in \mathfrak{L}$, and if there is also a link $\langle m.i, m.j.n.g.r.t \rangle \in \mathfrak{L}, f \neq g, i \neq j, |t| \geq 1$ then no link of the following types may appear:
(i) $\langle (m.j.n)^{<}h, m.j.n.g.(r.s)^{<}.u \rangle, |s| \geq 1$;
(ii) $\langle m.j.n.r^{<}h, m.j.n.r.s^{<}.u \rangle, |u| \geq 1$; and
(iii) $m.j.n.g.r.h$, may not appear in any other link, either as antecedent or as the foot of a link.

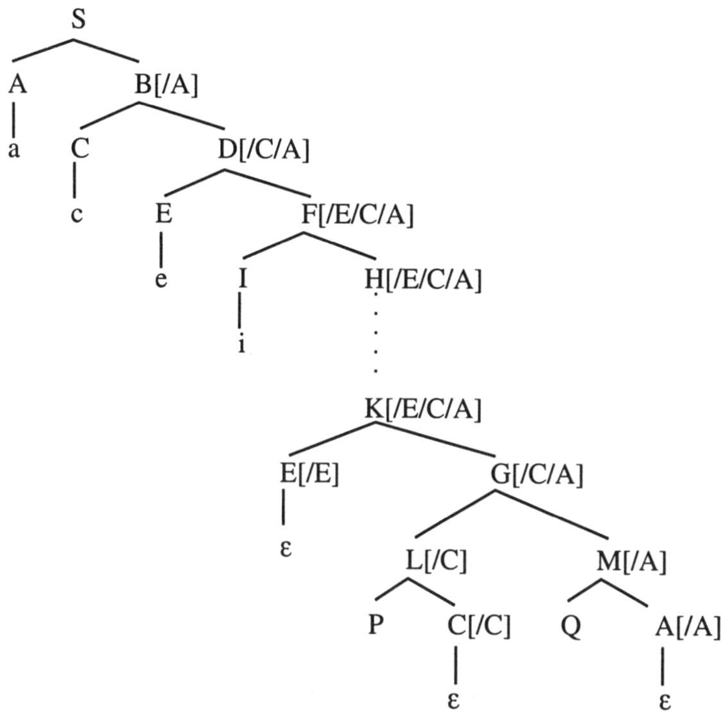

Figure 6.17

PROOF OF THEOREM (26).

If $\mathfrak{L}$ contains the link $\langle m.j.n.f, m.j.n.g.r.s\rangle$, then necessarily, a rule of type (20) was applied to node *m.j.n*, a rule of type (21b) or (22b) was applied to node $m.j.n.g.r.s^{-1}$, and rules of types (19), (20), (21b) or (22b) were applied to the nodes $\langle m.j.n.(g.r.s^{-1})^{<}$ on the path between those two nodes. If, moreover, $\mathfrak{L}$ contains a link $\langle m.i, m.j.n.g.r.t\rangle$, with $|t| \geq 1$ and such that the first element of t is not equal to the first element of s, then necessarily a rule of type (21b) or (22b) was applied to node *m.j.n.g.r*. This situation is illustrated in Figure 6.18, which will help follow the proof.

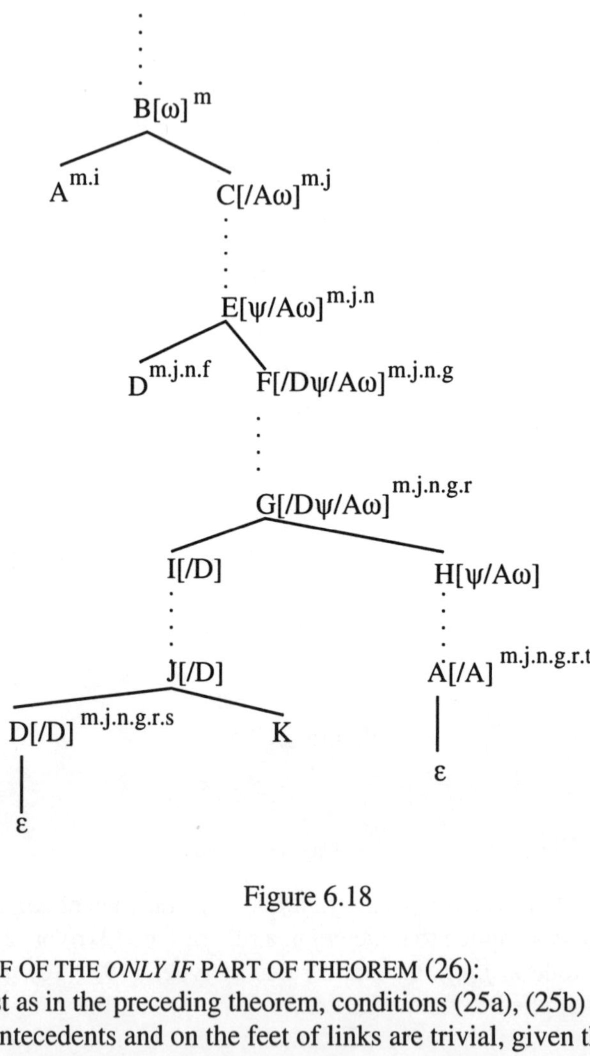

Figure 6.18

I. PROOF OF THE *ONLY IF* PART OF THEOREM (26):

Just as in the preceding theorem, conditions (25a), (25b) and (26iii) on the antecedents and on the feet of links are trivial, given the form of the rules authorized. Conditions (26i) and (26ii) result from the constraints on stack manipulation. A link of type (i) would require an index that was placed on the stack before another index (*/D* in Figure 6.18) to be popped before that index. Note that the presence of a third link (*/A* in Figure 6.18) is absolutely necessary for there to be a violation, since the form of rules (21b) and (22b) allows a popped index to continue its percolation downwards. In order to obtain a link of type (ii), it would be necessary to pop an index that was put on the stack after another index (*/D* in Figure 6.18) after the latter is popped. Once again, the presence of a third link is required for there to be a violation. ■

II. PROOF OF THE *IF* PART OF THEOREM (26):

Proof for this part of the theorem is once again similar to that given for the if part of theorem (13), except that in this case, it is condition (26) which ensures us that the constraints on pushing and popping indices of the stack are not violated, and that the necessary rules can thus be created. ■

6.7.4 Indexed Grammars of Type IGc

It is clear that grammars of the type IGb can generate trees of the type illustrated in Figure 6.17. Yet they cannot generate all the constructions necessary in order to account for unbounded dependencies in Swedish and Norwegian. Maling and Zaenen (1982: 265) give examples of sentences, the structure of which is illustrated in Figure 6.19, which clearly violate constraint (26), since they have 'crossing' links.[17] Figure 6.19 also shows how such structures can be accounted for with grammars of type IGc.

The easiest way to make clear what is meant here by 'crossing links' is to define them on trees of the type illustrated in Figure 6.19, rather than directly on constituent structures.[18] A tree has *n* crossing links if (i) there are *n* links which share a subpath in the paths from the filler to gap; this subpath will have an index stack with slashes for each of the *n* links; and (ii) the slash indices are popped off the stack in the same order as they were put on the stack (i.e. first in, first out), rather than the normal first in, last out order of IGs. In Figure 6.19, the shared subpath reduces to the single node labeled *F*[*/E/C/A*]. The indices are added to the stack and popped off the stack in the same order : *A*, *C*, *E*.[19]

---

[17] In these examples certain positions are actually occupied by resumptive pronouns instead of being empty. This is of no consequence for the present argumentation though (cf. Maling and Zaenen 1982 for detailed argumentation that these pronouns have the same status as gaps).

[18] It is possible to give a definition of crossing links directly on constituent structures, however I will not do so here because the required notation is cumbersome, and not very useful since no complete proof making use of it is provided.

[19] Nothing, of course, hinges on the procedural language used here: it is only present for purposes of clarity of exposition.

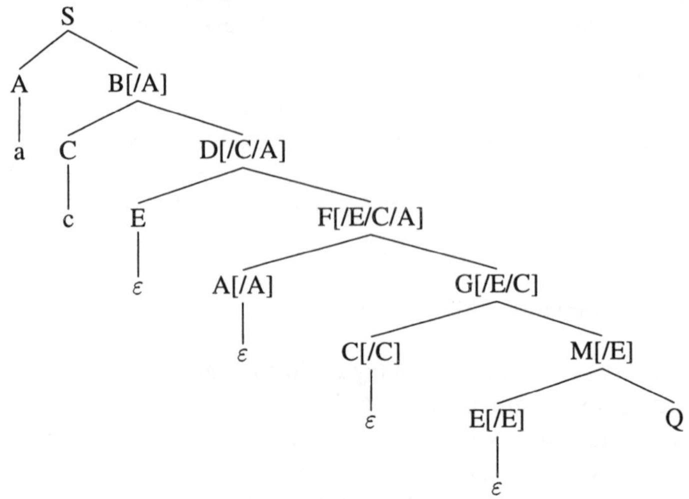

Figure 6.19

It is important to notice, moreover, that Maling and Zaenen, once again, give arguments to the effect that there is no competence limitation on the number of links that can be crossed in this way. If one accepts their position, which is based on an argument that has become classic since Chomsky and Miller 1963, one must conclude that even grammars of type IGc are not sufficient in SGC to account for these constructions, as the following theorem shows.[20]

---

[20] Note that indexed grammars can account for these sentences, which have linear linking systems (cf. footnote 3 above) of the type $a_1b_2c_3...\varepsilon_1\varepsilon_2\varepsilon_3...$ by assigning them the following structure:

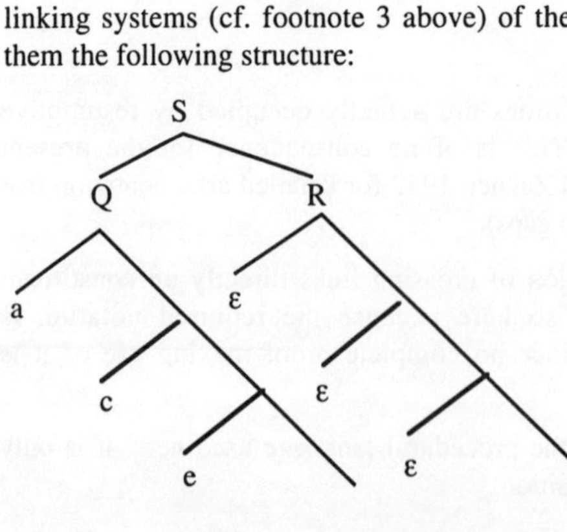

THEOREM

(27) For any language L generated by a grammar of type IGc G, there is an $n \geq 0$ such that for any derivation D in $\Sigma(G)$, the linking system defined by D has at most n crossing links.

The validity of this theorem can be easily seen. Notice that grammars of type IGc define crossing links by using rules of type (21c) and (22c), and that the maximum number of crossing links will be n if all the rules of this type have $i \leq n-1$. Since the number of productions is finite, such an n will exist for all grammars of this type.

In order to generate trees similar to the one in Figure 6.19, but without any limitation on the number of crossing links, one would have to be able to access the indices in an order that is different from that which is permitted by the grammars of type IGc. This would involve, e.g. interpreting the value of the SLASH feature as a multiset, rather than a stack, as is proposed in Pollard and Sag 1994.

6.7.5 Multisets as Values for SLASH Features

The consequences of allowing multisets of categories as the value of SLASH features is considerable, since it in effect allows unconstrained access to an unbounded memory store. This in principle leads to Turing capacity. In fact, such a system will remain within the bounds of context-sensitiveness if it observes a constraint to the effect that the maximal cardinality of the set of indices associated to any node in a tree is bounded by a linear function of the length of the terminal string of the tree. If this is true, it is possible to simulate the derivation on a linear bounded automaton. A restriction of this kind seems the minimal reasonable assumption. One would probably prefer some more powerful type of constraint.

6.8 Some Further Perspectives on Linking Systems

At the onset of this discussion of linking systems, it was mentioned that they could be applied to the characterization of other types of relations between constituents, such as agreement relations or anaphor-antecedent relations. Investigations similar to those conducted above on

---

But such a structure is entirely inadequate from an empirical point of view. This is an example of a situation where linear linking systems do not allow for a sufficiently detailed analysis of the capacities of a theory.

the expressibility of filler-gap dependencies in various frameworks should be conducted on the locality requirements imposed by various theories on agreement or anaphor-antecedent relations. In HPSG, for instance, this would involve discussing how the SUBCAT list mediates such relations, and what restrictions on locality this leads to (cf. e.g. Miller 1992: 229ff. for examples of attested agreement relations in natural languages which are in fact forbidden under the Pollard and Sag 1994 constraints). Another interesting constraint to be explored in this respect is Keenan's principle for possible agreement configurations (cf. Keenan 1974), which holds that items *A* and *B* can be an agreement target and an agreement trigger respectively if and only if the semantic translation of *A* is the argument of the semantic translation of *B*. Such a constraint imposes restrictions on the compatibility of linking systems and functor-argument structures. Detailed investigation of these matters must be left for future research.

Chapter 7

Conclusion

To conclude this study, I would like to compare the approach taken here with other recent work on the expressive power of linguistic formalisms, and to suggest some further avenues of research.

A first interesting article that can be taken to be a study of SGC is 'Category Structures' of Gazdar et al. 1988. They provide an abstract characterization of the notion of syntactic category, independently of any specific grammatical formalism, and analyze a series of frameworks, showing what classes of categories they are able to represent. Their work can be reinterpreted as providing an Interpretation Domain for the category systems adopted by various linguistic theories, as the following quote makes clear: "We do not concern ourselves with the appearance or representational details of a given theory of categories [...] but only with its underlying semantics — the issue of what set-theoretic (or other nonlinguistic) objects provide categories with their interpretations" (Gazdar et al. 1988, p.2). Specifically, one can interpret their space of categories K as forming an Interpretation Domain for Category Structures, with respect to which they characterize the SGC of various linguistic theories, via implicitly defined Interpretation Functions. For instance, one simple result obtained is that the theory of classical CFGs is strictly included with respect to category structures in the theory of standard GPSGs.

A second very important direction of research is that of Joshi and his collaborators, which has been centered on the University of Pennsylvania. Their study of the formal properties of TAGs and their comparison of those properties with those of other frameworks has led to very important work (see especially Vijay-Shanker 1987; Weir 1988; Becker, Joshi and Rambow 1991; Joshi and Schabes 1992; Rambow, Becker and Niv 1992, Rambow 1994, Rogers 1994). A summary of some of these results can be found in Joshi, Vijay-Shanker and Weir 1991. These studies provide important insights into the relationships between CFGs, TAGs, Linear Indexed Grammars (LIGs), Indexed Grammars (IGs), Head Grammars (HGs) and Combinatory Categorial Grammars (CCGs), and show how they can all be characterized as specifications of the general framework of Linear Context-Free Rewriting Systems (LCFRS). The initial thrust of this work was in characterizing relations in WGC between TAGs and other formalisms, but the types of constructions involved in creating proofs quickly gave rise to results concerning the classes of structural descriptions generable in the different formalisms. Some of these results, especially those concerning the expression of constituency, can be directly reinterpreted in terms of the framework provided here. For instance, HGs as characterized by Weir 1988 can be interpreted as defining discontinuous constituent structures, by contrast with LIGs and TAGs.[1] Interesting research remains to be conducted to determine exactly how the expressive capacity of HGs compares with that of the systems studied in section 4.2 in this respect.

Two specific ideas that have developed in the TAG literature, and are particularly relevant in the present context, the 'constant growth' property and the idea of 'derivational generative capacity'. One of the initial advantages that Joshi 1983 pointed out for TAGs was the fact that they have a constant growth property. Specifically, "a language L is said to possess the constant growth property iff there exists a constant M and a set of constants C such that for all sentences $w_k \in L$ with $|w_k| > M$, there exists another sentence in L, w_k', such that w_k is at most a constant longer than w_k', $|w_k| = |w_k'| + c$, for $c \in C$. A grammar is said to possess the constant growth property iff the language it generates is constant growth" (this version of the definition is from Berwick 1984, p.198). This interesting property, which is clearly a relevant interpretation for formalisms, and which is known to be shared by CFGs, TAGs, GPSGs, and by Berwick 1984's characterization of GB theory, but not by LFG as defined in Bresnan 1982, can be reinterpreted as follows in the terms of this study. We define an Interpretation Domain for length, $\mathrm{ID}_\ell = \mathrm{N}$, the set of natural numbers, and $\mathrm{IF}_{\mathrm{T}\rightarrow\ell}$ as a function which maps derivations in theory T onto the length of their terminal strings. For a grammar G in T, the properties of $\mathrm{IF}_{\mathrm{T}\rightarrow\ell}\,(\Sigma(G))$ will determine whether or not G is constant growth.

Second, and more important, is the notion of Derivational Generative Capacity introduced by Rambow, Becker and Niv 1992. The empirical basis of their discussion is a set of scrambling data from

---

[1] Note however that this reinterpretation is not a priori obvious, as the following quote shows: "Because TAG and HG are different systems, it is not possible to compare them with respect to their 'strong' generative capacity" Joshi, Vijay-Shanker and Weir 1991, p.56.

German, from which they conclude (pp.2-3) that German scrambling is 'doubly unbounded' in the following sense: (i) there is no bound on the distance over which each element can scramble; (ii) there is no bound on the number of unbounded dependencies that can occur in one sentence. On the basis of these data they show that no TAG (and more generally, no Linear Context-Free Rewriting Systems, LCFRS) can generate German, assigning structural descriptions such that a verb and its arguments are added in a single derivation step. This, they argue, shows that LCFRSs are inadequate in Derivational Generative Capacity for German scrambling data. Their analysis can be reinterpreted within the present framework using the interpretation domain for functor-argument structure introduced in section 5.1.4 of chapter 5 for categorial grammars. ID_{FA} was defined as the set of pairs $\langle S_1, \langle S_2, ..., S_n\rangle\rangle$, $n \geq 2$, where S_1 is the functor and $S_2, ..., S_n$ are its arguments. We define the Interpretation Function for functor-argument structure, $IF_{TAG \rightarrow FA}$, in such a way that only constituents contributed by a single elementary tree can be in a functor-argument structure. Under this analysis of the definition of functor-argument structure by TAGs, explicitly adopted by Rambow et al. (and under the obvious extension for LCFRSs) their proof shows that TAGs (and LCFRSs in general) cannot express pairs of interpretations in $\langle ID_{FA}, ID_O\rangle$ characterizing the full range of possibilities of German scrambling constructions (where ID_O is the Interpretation Domain for linear ordering of occurrences). It should be noted however, that the idea that the constituents involved in a functor-argument relation should be contributed by a 'single derivational step' is not a generally plausible constraint, especially in other frameworks than TAGs. It is clear that frameworks like GPSG, LFG or CG should be interpreted as expressing such relations between items that do *not* satisfy this constraint.

Finally, I would like to point out that the framework for the study of SGC developed here has a much broader applicability than the domain of syntax, with respect to which it has been illustrated. It can clearly be extended to other components of grammar, such as phonology, morphology and semantics. Some notions such as constituency, dependency and order have obvious correlates in phonology and morphology, and it would be interesting to study the expressive power of theories of these components in those respects. Similarly, the concept of function-argument structure is crucial to semantics. Moreover, beyond the Interpretation Domains discussed here, new Domains should be designed to capture specific intended interpretations of these other components of grammatical theory. One interesting example in this regard would be an Interpretation Domain for denotational semantics, ID_{DS}, consisting e.g. in the set of well-formed formulas of Montague's intensional logic. Remarkably, there has in fact been a study which is specifically relevant to this question. Cooper and Parsons 1976 gave a proof which amounts to showing that three different grammars, written in three different theoretical frameworks, are equivalent in SGC with respect to denotational semantics, in the sense of section 3.6.1.1. They showed that there are bijections between the derivation sets of the three grammars (with minor caveats, which are unimportant given the way we define equivalence in SGC between grammars in section 3.6.1.1, which doesn't require one-to-one correspondence) such that derivations related by the bijections are mapped onto the same element in the Interpretation Domain for denotational semantics. Specifically, they define a first grammar using a transformational syntax (C(ooper) syntax), which generates the same sentences as Montague's PTQ syntax (M-syntax), and a bijective mapping between the sets of M-derivations and C-derivations generated. They provide a semantics that translates the deep structures of C-syntax into Montague's intensional logic. This is in effect the relevant Interpretation Function $IF_{C \rightarrow DS}$ into ID_{DS} for C-syntax. Finally, they prove that corresponding derivations in C-syntax and M-syntax are mapped onto the same translation in intensional logic respectively by $IF_{C \rightarrow DS}$ and by Montague's rules of semantic interpretation, which constitute the relevant $IF_{M \rightarrow DS}$ for M-syntax. Finally, they prove the same property for a third grammar with a syntax closer to that of 'interpretative semantics'.

Obviously, this very interesting result has a limited scope, since it concerns only the existence of equivalent grammars in the different formalisms, but gives no information as to the range of possibilities offered by each of the theories, and how they compare. There clearly remains significant work to be done in this domain. For example, it would be interesting to compare the range of possibilities of quantification in theories of semantics involving quantifier raising in LF (e.g. May 1985), and the classical 'quantifying in' strategies of PTQ.[2]

The use of syntactic illustrations in this study has led to a further bias, which it is interesting to clarify. From the syntactic perspective, the idea that utterances are linearly arranged sequences of units has a certain obviousness, which explains the compelling status of the idea of WGC, as the set of strings generated by a grammar. However, stepping back

---

[2] As suggested to me by David Dowty (p.c.).

from this syntactic viewpoint, we can conceive of an utterance in a much more abstract way, as an entity which has interpretations on the phonological level as a collection of phonological events (cf. Bird and Klein 1990) and on the semantic level as a formula of intensional logic, for example. Both of these levels lend themselves to subanalyses into a variety of relevant interpretations. On the syntactic level one of the relevant interpretations of an utterance, beyond those that we have discussed, is the corresponding sequence of syntactic word level units. In effect, this simply assimilates the notion of string of syntactic words, and the classical notion of WGC based upon it, to one further relevant Interpretation Domain in our relativistic multidimensional view of SGC. Under this analysis, the WGC of a grammar is simply its SGC with respect to the Interpretation Domain for strings of syntactic words, with Interpretation Functions for WGC mapping structural descriptions in the grammar to the string of syntactic words they define.

References

Ades, Anthony and Mark J. Steedman. 1982. On the order of words. *Linguistics and Philosophy* 4: 517-558.

Aho, Alfred V. 1988. Indexed grammars. *Journal of the ACM* 15: 647-671.

Ajdukiewicz, Kazimierz. 1935. Die syntaktische Konnexität. *Studia Philosophica* 1: 1-27. Translated in *Polish Logic 1920-1939*, edited by S. McCall, 207-231, Oxford: Oxford University Press, 1967.

Bar-Hillel, Yehoshua, Haïm Gaifman, and E. Shamir. 1964. On categorial and phrase structure grammars. In *Language and Information*, edited by Y. Bar-Hillel. Reading, MA: Addison-Wesley, 99-115. First published in *Bulletin of the Research Council of Israel* (1960):1-16.

Barker, Chris and Geoffrey K. Pullum. 1990. A theory of command relations. *Linguistics and Philosophy* 13.1: 1-34.

Becker, Tilman, Aravind K. Joshi, and Owen Rambow. 1991. Long-distance scrambling and tree adjoining grammars. *Proceedings of the 5th Conference of the European Chapter of the Association of Computational Linguistics*, Vol. 5: 21-26.

Berwick, Robert C. 1984. Strong generative capacity, weak generative capacity and modern linguistic theories. *Computational Linguistics* 10.3-4: 189-202.

Berwick, Robert C. and Amy S. Weinberg. 1984. *The Grammatical Basis of Linguistic Performance*. Cambridge, MA: MIT Press.

Bird, Steven and Ewan Klein. 1990. Phonological events. *Journal of Linguistics* 26: 33-56.

Bloomfield, Leonard. 1933. *Language*. London: George Allen and Unwin.

Bresnan, Joan W. 1976. On the form and functioning of transformations. *Linguistic Inquiry* 7: 3-40.

Bresnan, Joan W., ed. 1982. *The Mental Representation of Grammatical Relations*. Cambridge, MA: MIT Press.

Chomsky, Noam. 1957. *Syntactic Structures*. The Hague: Mouton.

Chomsky, Noam. 1963. Formal properties of grammar. In *Handbook of Mathematical Psychology*, vol. II, edited by R.D. Luce, R.R. Bush, and E. Galanter, 323-418. New York: Wiley.

Chomsky, Noam. 1965. *Aspects of the Theory of Syntax*. Cambridge, MA: MIT Press.

Chomsky, Noam. 1970. Remarks on nominalization. In *Readings in English Transformational Grammar*, edited by R.A. Jacobs and P.S. Rosenbaum, 184-221, Waltham, MA: Ginn.

Chomsky, Noam. 1973. Conditions on transformations. In *A Festschrift for Morris Halle*, edited by S. Anderson and P. Kiparsky, 232-286. New York: Holt, Rinehart and Winston.

Chomsky, Noam. 1986. *Barriers*. Cambridge, MA: MIT Press.

Chomsky, Noam and George A. Miller. 1963. Introduction to the formal analysis of natural languages. In *Handbook of Mathematical Psychology*, vol. II, edited by R.D. Luce, R.R. Bush, and E. Galanter, 269-322. New York: Wiley.

Cooper, Robin, and Terence Parsons. 1976. Montague Grammar, Generative Semantics and Interpretative Semantics. In *Montague Grammar*, edited by B. Partee, 311-362. New York: Academic Press.

Desclés, Jean-Pierre. 1990. *Langages applicatifs, langues naturelles et cognition*. Paris: Hermès.

Dominicy, Marc. 1982. Condillac et les grammaires de dépendance. In *Condillac et les problèmes du langage*, edited by J. Sgard, 313-343. Genève: Slatkine.

Dowty, David R. 1996. Toward a minimalist theory of syntactic structure. In *Discontinuous Constituency*, edited by H.C. Bunt and A. Van Horck. Berlin: Mouton de Gruyter .

Dowty, David R., Robert E. Wall, and Stanley Peters. 1981. *Introduction to Montague Semantics*. Dordrecht: Reidel.

Friedman, Joyce D., Dawei Dai, and Weiguo Wang. 1986. The weak generative capacity of parenthesis free categorial grammars. *Proceedings of Coling '86*: 199-201.

Gaifman, Chaïm. 1965. Dependency systems and phrase structure systems. *Information and Control* 8: 304-337.

Gallier, Jean H. 1986. *Logic for Computer Science*. New York: Harper and Row.

Gazdar, Gerald. 1988. Applicability of indexed grammars to natural languages. In *Natural Language Parsing and Linguistic Theories*, edited by U. Reyle and C. Rohrer, 69-94. Dordrecht: Reidel.

Gazdar, Gerald, Ewan Klein, Geoffrey K. Pullum, and Ivan A. Sag. 1985. *Generalized Phrase Structure Grammar*. Cambridge, MA: Harvard University Press.

Gazdar, Gerald and Geoffrey K. Pullum. 1981. Subcategorization, constituent order, and the notion of 'head'. In *The Scope of Lexical Rules*, edited by M. Moortgat, H. van der Hulst, and T. Hoekstra, 107-123. Dordrecht, Foris.

Gazdar, Gerald, Geoffrey K. Pullum, Robert Carpenter, Ewan Klein, Thomas E. Hukari, and Robert D. Levine. 1988. Category structures. *Computational Linguistics* 14.1: 1-19.

Gladkii, A.V. 1970. *Leçons de linguistique mathématique*. Paris: Dunod.

Harris, Zellig S. 1951. *Structural Linguistics*. Chicago: University of Chicago Press.

Harris, Zellig S. 1962. *String Analysis of Sentence Structure*. The Hague: Mouton.

Hays, David G. 1964. Dependency theory: a formalism and some observations. *Language* 40: 511-525.

Higginbotham 1983. A note on phrase-markers. *Revue Québecoise de Linguistique* 13: 147-166.

Hoeksema, Jack. 1991. Complex predicates and liberation in Dutch and English. *Linguistics and Philosophy* 14.6: 661-710.

Huck, Geoffrey J. and Almerindo E. Ojeda. 1987. *Syntax and Semantics 20: Discontinuous Constituency*. Orlando: Academic Press.

Hudson, Richard. 1984. *Word Grammar*. Oxford: Blackwell.

Joshi, Aravind K. 1983. Factoring recursion and dependencies: an aspect of tree adjoining grammars (TAG) and a comparison of some formal properties of TAGs, GPSGs, PLGs, and LPGs. *Proceedings of the 21st Annual Meeting of the ACL*: 7-15.

Joshi, Aravind K. 1985. Tree adjoining grammars: How much context-sensitivity is required to provide reasonable structural descriptions. In *Natural Language Parsing*, edited by D. Dowty, L. Karttunen, and A. M. Zwicky, 206-250. Cambridge: Cambridge University Press.

Joshi, Aravind K. 1987. An introduction to tree adjoining grammars. In *Mathematics of Language*, edited by A. Manaster-Ramer, 87-114. Amsterdam: John Benjamins.

Joshi, Aravind K., S.R. Kosaraju, and H.M. Yamada. 1972. String adjunct grammars, parts I and II. *Information and Control* 21: 93-116 and 235-260.

Joshi, Aravind K. and Yves Schabes. 1992. Tree-Adjoining Grammars and lexicalized grammars. In *Tree Automata and Languages*, edited by M. Nivat and A. Podelski, 409-431. Amsterdam: Elsevier.

Joshi, Aravind K. and Yves Schabes. 1997. Tree Adjoining Grammars. In *Handbook of Formal Languages and Automata*, Vol. 3, edited by A. Salomma and G. Rosenberg. Heidelberg: Springer-Verlag.

Joshi, Aravind K., K. Vijay-Shanker, and David J. Weir. 1991. The convergence of mildly context-sensitive grammar formalisms. In *Foundational Issues in Natural Language Processing*, edited by P. Sells, S. Shieber, and T. Wasow, 31-81. Cambridge, MA: MIT Press.

Kaplan, Ronald M. and Annie Zaenen. 1989. Long-distance dependencies, constituent structure and functional uncertainty. In *Alternative Conceptions of Constituent Structure*, edited by M. Baltin and A. Kroch, 17-42. Chicago: Chicago University Press.

Keenan, E. 1974. The functional principle: generalizing the notion of 'subject-of'. *Papers from the 10th Regional Meeting of the Chicago Linguistic Society*: 298-309.

Kornai, András and Geoffrey K. Pullum. 1990. The X-bar theory of phrase structure. *Language* 66.1: 24-50.

Kuroda, S.-Y. 1973. Généralisation de la notion d'équivalence de grammaires: une méthode topologique. In *The Formal Analysis of Natural Languages*, edited by M. Gross, M. Halle, and M.-P. Schützenberger, 362-371. The Hague: Mouton.

Kuroda, S.-Y. 1976. A topological study of phrase structure languages. *Information and Control* 30: 307-379.

Kuroda, S.-Y. 1987. A topological approach to structural equivalence of formal languages. In *Mathematics of Language*, edited by A. Manaster-Ramer, 173-189. Amsterdam: John Benjamins.

Langendoen, D. Terence. 1976. On the weak generative capacity of infinite grammars, *CUNY Forum* 1: 13-24.

Levelt, W.J.M. 1974. *Formal Grammars in Linguistics and Psycholinguistics. Vol. II Applications in Linguistic Theory*. The Hague: Mouton.

McCawley, James D. 1982. Parentheticals and discontinuous constituent structure. *Linguistic Inquiry* 13.1: 91-106.

McCawley, James D. 1987. Some additional evidence for discontinuity. In *Syntax and Semantics 20: Discontinuous Constituency*, edited by G. Huck and A. Ojeda, 185-200. Orlando: Academic Press.

Maling, Joan and Annie Zaenen. 1982. Scandinavian extraction phenomena. In *The Nature of Syntactic Representation*, edited by P. Jacobson and G.K. Pullum, 229-282. Dordrecht: Reidel.

Manaster-Ramer, Alexis. 1987a. Dutch as a formal language. *Linguistics and Philosophy* 10: 221-246.

Marcus, Mitchell P., Donald Hindle, and Margaret M. Fleck. 1983. D-Theory: Talking about talking about trees. *Proceedings of the 21 Annual Meeting of the ACL*: 129-136.

Marcus, Solomon. 1967. *Introduction mathématique à la linguistique structurale*. Paris: Dunod.

May, Robert. 1985. *Logical Form*. Cambridge, MA: MIT Press.

Mel'čuk, Igor A. and Nikolaj V. Pertsov. 1987. *Surface Syntax of English. A Formal Model within the Meaning-text Framework*. Amsterdam: Benjamins.

Miller, Philip H. 1983. *La comparaison des théories linguistiques formalisées avec une application aux problèmes du syntagme nominal*. Unpublished mémoire de licence, Université libre de Bruxelles.

Miller, Philip H. 1986-7. On the formalization of string analysis, parts I and II. *The Prague Bulletin of Mathematical Linguistics* 46: 13-40 and 47: 3-23.

Miller, Philip H. 1990. Les systèmes de liage. In *Formalismes syntaxiques pour le traitement automatique du langage naturel*, edited by P.H. Miller and T. Torris, 207-243. Paris: Hermès.

Miller, Philip H. 1991. Scandinavian extraction phenomena revisited: weak and strong generative capacity. *Linguistics and Philosophy* 14.1: 101-113.

Miller, Philip H. 1992. *Clitics and Constituent in Phrase Structure Grammar*. New York: Garland.

Miller, Philip H. 1993. A semantic analysis of strong generative capacity. In *Proceedings of the 9th Amsterdam Colloquium*, edited by P. Dekker et M. Stokhof, 411-426. Amsterdam: University of Amsterdam, ILLC/Department of Philosophy.

Milner, Jean-Claude. 1989. *Introduction à une science du langage*. Paris: Le Seuil.

Montague, Richard. 1974. Universal Grammar. In *Formal Philosophy*, edited by R. H. Thomason, 222-246. New Haven, Connecticut: Yale University Press.

Moortgat, Michael. 1989. *Categorial Investigations: Logical and Linguistic Aspects of the Lambek Calculus*. Dordrecht: Foris.

Ojeda, Almerindo E. 1987. Discontinuity, multidominance, and unbounded dependency in generalized phrase structure grammar: some preliminaries. In *Syntax and Semantics 20: Discontinuous Constituency*, edited by G. Huck and A. Ojeda, 257-282. Orlando: Academic Press.

Ojeda, Almerindo E. 1988. A linear precedence account of cross-serial dependencies. *Linguistics and Philosophy* 11.4: 457-492.

Ortiz de Urbina, Jon. 1989. *Parameter in the Grammar of Basque: A GB Approach to Basque Syntax.* Dordrecht: Foris.

Peters, P.S. and R.W. Ritchie. 1973. On the generative power of transformational grammars, *Information Sciences* 6: 49-83.

Peters, P.S. and R.W. Ritchie. 1982. Phrase linking grammars. Unpublished paper, University of Texas at Austin.

Pollard, Carl and Ivan A. Sag. 1994. *Head-Driven Phrase Structure Grammar.* Chicago: Chicago University Press.

Pullum, Geoffrey K. 1982. Free word order and phrase structure rules. *Proceedings of NELS* 12: 209-220.

Pullum, Geoffrey K. 1989. *Strong Generative Capacity and Unrestricted Rewriting Systems.* Unpublished manuscript, University of California, Santa Cruz.

Pullum, Geoffrey K. 1991. English nominal gerund phrases as noun phrases with verb phrase heads. *Linguistics* 29: 763-799.

Rambow, Owen. 1994. *Formal and Computational Aspects of Natural Language Syntax.* Unpublished PhD Dissertation, University of Pennsylvania, IRCS Report 94-08.

Rambow, Owen, Tilman Becker, and Michael Niv. 1992. *The derivational generative power of formal systems or Scrambling is beyond LCFRS.* Paper presented at the Third Mathematics of Language Workshop (MOL3), Austin, Texas.

Reape, Mike. 1994. Domain union and word order variation in German. In *German in Head-Driven Phrase Structure Grammar*, edited by J. Nerbonne, K. Netter, and C. Pollard, 151-197. Stanford: CSLI publications.

Robinson, Jane J. 1970. Dependency structures and transformational rules. *Language* 46: 259-285.

Rogers, James. 1994. *Studies in the Logic of Trees with Applications to Grammar Formalisms.* Unpublished dissertation, University of Delaware, Technical report 95-04

Rounds, William C., Alexis Manaster-Ramer, and Joyce Friedman. 1987. Finding natural languages a home in formal language theory. In *Mathematics of Language*, edited by A. Manaster-Ramer, 349-359. Amsterdam: John Benjamins.

Sag, Ivan A., Thomas Wasow, Gerald Gazdar, and Steven Weisler. 1985. Coordination and how to distinguish categories. *Natural Language and Linguistic Theory* 3: 117-171.

Stabler, Edward P. Jr. 1992. *The Logical Approach to Syntax.* Cambridge, MA: MIT Press.

Steedman, Mark. 1985. Dependency and coordination in the grammar of Dutch and English. *Language* 61.3: 523-568.

Tesnière, L. 1959. *Eléments de syntaxe structurale.* Paris: Klincksieck.

Thatcher, J.W. 1973. Tree automata: an informal survey. In *Currents in the Theory of Computing*, edited by A.V. Aho, 143-172. Englewood Cliffs, NJ: Prentice Hall.

Vijayashanker, K. 1987. *A Study of Tree Adjoining Grammars.* Unpublished Ph.D. Dissertation. University of Pennsylvania.

Weir, David J. 1988. *Characterizing Mildly Context-Sensitive Grammar Formalisms.* Unpublished Ph.D. Dissertation, University of Pennsylvania.

Williams, Edwin S. 1981. Language acquisition, markedness, and phrase structure. In *Language Acquisition and Linguistic Theory* edited by S. L.Tavakolian, 8-34. Cambridge, MA: MIT Press.

Zwicky, Arnold M. 1986. Concatenation and Liberation. *Proceedings of CLS 22*: 65-94.

Zwicky, Arnold M. and Geoffrey K. Pullum. 1986. The principle of phonology-free syntax: introductory remarks. *OSU WPL* 32: 63-91.

Index of Subjects and Abbreviations

Index of Names